The Broken Promise of Global Advocacy

The Broken Promise of Global Advocacy addresses two key normative debates associated with the rise of transnational advocacy: whether global interest communities are biased in favor of wealthier countries, and whether the growth of global advocacy implies the emergence of a global civil society truly representative of global constituencies.

The authors address these important debates using original data drawn from a large-scale project which maps all organized interests participating in two international venues: the World Trade Organization's Ministerial Conferences (1995–2017) and the United Nations Climate Summits (1997–2017). They leverage this unique dataset to carry out a systematic empirical assessment of contending views on the factors driving the rise of transnational advocacy. In doing so, the book demonstrates that cross-national differences in global interest representation largely mirror states' economic power and that global interest communities are likely to remain dominated by organizations representing national – rather than global – interests.

This book will be of great interest to students and scholars working in comparative politics, public policy, governance, international relations, and international political economy.

Marcel Hanegraaff is Associate Professor in the Department of Political Science at the University of Amsterdam, the Netherlands.

Arlo Poletti is Associate Professor in the Department of Sociology and Social Research at the University of Trento, Italy.

Innovations in International Affairs

Series Editor: Raffaele Marchetti, *LUISS Guido Carli, Italy*

Innovations in International Affairs aims to provide cutting-edge analyses of controversial trends in international affairs with the intent to innovate our understanding of global politics. Hosting mainstream as well as alternative stances, the series promotes both the re-assessment of traditional topics and the exploration of new aspects.

The series invites both engaged scholars and reflective practitioners, and is committed to bringing non-western voices into current debates.

Innovations in International Affairs is keen to consider new book proposals in the following key areas:

- **Innovative topics**: related to aspects that have remained marginal in scholarly and public debates
- **International crises**: related to the most urgent contemporary phenomena and how to interpret and tackle them
- **World perspectives**: related mostly to non-western points of view

Titles in this series include:

International and Local Actors in Disaster Response
Responding to the Beirut Explosion
Tania N. Haddad

The Broken Promise of Global Advocacy
Inequality in Global Interest Representation
Marcel Hanegraaff and Arlo Poletti

For more information about this series, please visit: https://www.routledge.com/Innovations-in-International-Affairs/book-series/IIA

The Broken Promise of Global Advocacy

Inequality in Global Interest Representation

Marcel Hanegraaff and Arlo Poletti

Routledge
Taylor & Francis Group

LONDON AND NEW YORK

First published 2023
by Routledge
4 Park Square, Milton Park, Abingdon, Oxon OX14 4RN

and by Routledge
605 Third Avenue, New York, NY 10158

Routledge is an imprint of the Taylor & Francis Group, an informa business

British Library Cataloguing-in-Publication Data
A catalogue record for this book is available from the British Library

Library of Congress Cataloging-in-Publication Data
A catalog record has been requested for this book

ISBN: 978-1-032-16029-0 (hbk)
ISBN: 978-1-032-16030-6 (pbk)
ISBN: 978-1-003-24679-4 (ebk)

DOI: 10.4324/9781003246794

Typeset in Times New Roman
by Deanta Global Publishing Services, Chennai, India

Contents

Preface

This book is a product of our long-time collaboration in academia. Since we met – at the University of Antwerp somewhere in the early 2010s – we have worked together on various papers and projects. This book ties together in a coherent manner many of our previous theoretical and empirical contributions. Our main message is not optimistic: we see the rise of global advocacy as inherently flawed and mostly benefitting already powerful nations and actors. This stands in sharp contrast to the more optimistic accounts associated with the opening up of international organizations (IOs) during the mid-1990s. Considering what we know from advocacy in domestic political systems, this conclusion should come as no surprise. Advocacy is to a large extent driven by the availability of resources. To put it simply: more money mostly means that organizations develop more effective advocacy campaigns, which usually leads to more impact on decision-making procedures.

This view stands in contrast to institutional approaches which focus on the role of international organizations (IOs) as important facilitators of non-state actor mobilization. We do not doubt the good intentions of these organizations in wanting to create a level playing field for the many non-state actors participating at these venues. Yet, we do question the effectiveness of their efforts. More resourceful organizations will find a way to adapt to institutional demands in a more effective way compared to less resourceful organizations, leading them to benefit more from their participation in these global governance institutions. This is a difficult – but crucial –conclusion that we draw. It should lead us to rethink how IOs involve non-state actors in their activities with a view to increasing inclusiveness and equality.

During all these years, much of the theoretical and empirical contents of this book have been discussed at various conferences, workshops, and seminars. We are grateful to all the colleagues who offered their input on these various occasions. It is impossible to provide a detailed list of all these colleagues, and we would like to thank here those among them who read and commented on earlier research drafts on which the manuscript builds. We want to single out one person who has contributed the most to this project: Jan Beyers of the University of Antwerp. Most of the empirical works presented in this book stem from the PhD project of Marcel Hanegraaff, one of Jan's former PhD students, and this project would simply not have existed without the generous support he provided throughout the years. On the one hand, this support was financial, allowing Marcel Hanegraaff to build a large dataset on global advocacy (indeed, in academia the availability of resources is also a critical factor for success!). On the other hand, this support came in the form of providing academic guidance: without the critical, but supportive, comments Jan provided over the years, all the papers related to this topic, let alone this book, would have likely not materialized. Many thanks for his continued support.

We would also like to gratefully acknowledge the financial support of the Research Council of the University of Antwerp. We would also like to thank the Research Foundation-Flanders (Odysseus Program, project number G.0908.09) and the European Research Council (ERC-2013-CoG 616702-iBias) for their financial contributions. For both projects Jan Beyers was the principal investigator and many of the ideas proposed in this book would have never existed without these projects.

On a more personal note, Marcel Hanegraaff would like to thank his wife Danielle for her continuous and patient support, and he would like to dedicate this research endeavor to his daughter Emma and his son Lars. Emma always wanted to see herself referenced in a book, so one of her dreams has now become a reality. I hope this is just the start of all her dreams coming true.

Amsterdam and Trento,
February 2022

Introduction

In the past decades, to a greater or lesser extent, virtually all economic, political, and social activities have become subjected to rules decided upon, implemented, monitored, and enforced by international institutions of various sorts. The nation-state has not gone out of business, but it is beyond doubt that an increasing number of regulatory processes traditionally confined within its boundaries have today been complemented by new forms of policy-making taking place within a wide array of different international institutional venues. Areas as diverse as trade, finance, the environment, human rights, and even national security are more and more subjected to rules developed under the auspices of international governance systems (Mattli and Woods 2009).

As global governance systems have become increasingly relevant in contemporary policy-making, the number and scope of organized interests that mobilize beyond national borders have also risen dramatically. As a result, transnational advocacy by domestic and global non-state actors has become a key feature of the politics of global governance across different institutional venues (Beckfield 2003; Hanegraaff 2015; Nordang-Uhre 2014; Schroeder et al. 2012; Smith and Weist 2005; Steffeck et al. 2008; Tallberg et al. 2013; Tallberg et al. 2014). This trend is not surprising. On the one hand, the nesting of states within increasingly influential sets of global governance systems created obvious incentives for various kinds of non-state actors to mobilize on a transnational basis (Barnett and Finnemore 2004; Beckfield 2003; Meyer 1980; Tallberg et al. 2013). On the other hand, transnational advocacy was further stimulated by far-reaching institutional transformations enabling a systematic shift toward greater involvement of non-state actors in global governance (Tallberg et al. 2013; Tallberg et al. 2014).

The rapidly growing involvement of non-state actors that mobilize on a transnational basis initially came with – at least – two optimistic expectations regarding the equality and democratic nature of global decision-making.

DOI: 10.4324/9781003246794-1

The first relates to this phenomenon's effects on *North–South inequalities*. The initial thought was that the growth of transnational advocacy would lead global governance to become more representative of and accessible to all the world's citizens by empowering the interests of the global South. Despite optimistic expectations, the empirical reality paints a more mixed picture. While many have highlighted that the growth of transnational advocacy has the potential to make global governance more representative of and accessible to all the world's citizens (Barnett and Finnemore 2004; Boli and Thomas 1997, 1999), others have expressed concerns about the possibility that such a quantitative growth of transnationally mobilized non-state actors might end up reproducing or even exacerbating representational asymmetries at the global level. More specifically, scholars have increasingly worried about the possibility that the steady growth of transnational advocacy may turn out to widen representational inequalities between the so-called North and the South, ultimately making global governance even more skewed in favor of the interests of wealthier countries at the expense of developing ones (Beckfield 2003; Chase-Dunn et al. 2000; Smith and Weist 2005; Zürn 2014). At this point the jury is therefore still out on whether the inclusion of non-state actors benefits the global South or North more.

A second optimistic expectation relates to the democratic legitimacy of global decision-making procedures, because transnational advocacy could potentially trigger the development of a *global public sphere* based on a fair representation of relevant global constituencies. Whether or not a global public sphere has indeed emerged remains to be ascertained empirically. Does the rise of transnational advocacy mean that a truly global civil society is finally gaining representation in global governance? Or, is it contributing to making nation-level constituencies and interests even more central in global governance? Addressing this debate is crucial to understanding the potential of stakeholder strategies for the democratization of global governance (Dellmuth and Tallberg 2015; Hanegraaff and Poletti 2018). Different variants of stakeholder theory concur in stressing that such strategies can be effective only as long as they enable the interests of relevant global constituencies to be effectively represented alongside the interests of national ones. For instance, Patrizia Nanz and Jens Steffek (2005) argue that opening up global governance to greater participation by non-state actors can generate democratic legitimacy only if it leads to the emergence of institutionalized arenas for deliberative participation beyond the limits on national boundaries. Jan Aarte Scholte (2004) similarly argues that making global governance democratically legitimate requires overcoming nationalist structures of community and give meaningful representation to increasingly important cosmopolitan bonds and trans-border solidarities. Manuel Castells (2008) also contends that meeting the challenges of democratic legitimacy in the current global order requires giving voice to a truly global civil society. To put it differently, it is just eminently plausible that a global socio-political order that remains defined by the realpolitik of nation-states, rather than by stakeholders that can enhance broader transnational debates, can hardly be expected to generate political processes that can be perceived as democratically legitimate (Held 2004).

Underlying these two normative debates are two broad theoretical perspectives on the factors that matter most in determining and shaping the rise of transnational advocacy. One perspective focuses on the *political opportunities* that the global political arena provides for the political mobilization of non-state actors and the consequences that these opportunities engender (Hanegraaff et al. 2015; Hanegraaff et al. 2017). In the context of the analysis of transnational lobbying, this 'demand-side' perspective largely stresses the potential effects brought about by the opening up of global governance arenas to the input of various kinds of non-state actors. Such perspective deems institutional reforms aimed at increasing access opportunities for non-state actors' participation in global governance as a crucial factor determining not only the quantitative growth of transnational lobbying but also its quality. If it is true that political institutional structures matter a great deal in shaping patterns of political mobilization of organized interests, then institutional reforms that increase non-state actors' access to these international institutions could be designed to effectively reduce North–South inequalities in global interest representation or to trigger the emergence of a truly global civil society. More or less explicitly, stakeholder strategies of democratization of global governance rely on this perspective. Stakeholder models of democracy posit that increasing democratic legitimacy of a particular political system increases when all the actors affected by decisions produced within the system are given the opportunity to meaningfully participate and make their voice heard in the making of such decisions (Macdonald 2008; Macdonald and Macdonald 2006). The unstated assumption of these approaches is that greater access opportunities for stakeholders will eventually translate into greater participation by stakeholders previously excluded from the policy-making process and stimulate international deliberation\s among a wide range of state actors and non-state actors.

Another perspective emphasizes that non-state actors' *capacity* to become politically active is crucially influenced by their capacity to obtain resources for the direct environment in which they operate (Gray and Lowery 1996; Lowery and Gray 2004; Hanegraaff et al. 2015; Hanegraaff and Poletti 2017, 2020; Nownes 2010; Nownes and Lipinski 2005). Views diverge as to what types of resources matter more in triggering the mobilization of non-state actors. Some point to the importance of the size of an economy, suggesting a correlation between GDP and organized interests' activism (e.g., Berkhout et al. 2018; Carroll and Rasmussen 2017; Hanegraaff and Poletti 2020; Messer et al. 2011), while others focus on differences in the levels of development across different economies, suggesting a correlation between a GNI per capita and transnational activism (e.g., Bailer et al. 2013; Beckfield 2003; Bischoff 2003; Coates et al. 2007; Lee 2010; Nordang Uhre 2014; Rasmussen and Alexandrova 2012; Smith 2005; Smith and Wiest 2005). Irrespective of these important differences, these 'supply-side' perspectives suggest that the development of transnational organized interest communities co-varies with the overall resource base that is potentially accessible to domestic non-state actors. More economically and socially developed states will have more extensive and diversified interest group communities at the domestic level, which should then translate into higher levels of representation in global governance where costs of collective action are even higher than in the national context. Thus, according to this view, more openness in global governance will not trigger the participation of formerly excluded non-state actors but, rather, further strengthen patterns of disproportional participation favoring non-state actors from resourceful countries. Moreover, this view suggests that a truly global public sphere is unlikely to arise because global advocacy will remain dominated by the non-state actors representing national, rather than global, interests.

In this book we aim to address these normative and theoretical debates by carrying out a large-scale and systematic empirical assessment of the effects of the opening up to the input of non-state actors of two key international organizations (IOs). More specifically, we focus on non-state actors' participation at the World Trade Organization (WTO) and at the United Nations Framework Convention on Climate Change (UNFCCC). First, we collected and coded information on the participation of non-state actors in both venues since such participation was authorized. Second, we rely on additional information on these non-state actors obtained through extensive interviews. In total our data covers over 10,000 unique non-state actors: around 2,000 at the WTO since 1995 and more than 8,000 at the UNFCCC since 1997. Third, we rely on interview survey data with around 600 non-state actor representatives collected at various WTO Ministerial Conferences and UNFCCC's Conference of the Parties. Finally, we also make use of interview data with almost 400 delegates active at these conferences. Based on this unprecedented dataset we focus on two sets of broad questions: whether the growth of transnational lobbying *reduced North–South* inequalities and the extent to which such a phenomenon triggered the emergence of a *global public sphere*.

In each chapter we focus on a different aspect of the two broad questions discussed above. In particular, we devote two chapters to each issue.

While Chapters 2 and 3 discuss different sets of empirical evidence on the effects of global advocacy on North–South inequalities in global interest representation, Chapters 4 and 5 are devoted to assess whether strengthened opportunities for stakeholder involvement succeeded in enabling greater representation of global constituencies, thus triggering the emergence of a truly global public sphere.

In general, our findings support two broad sets of observations, both of which lend credence to a 'supply-side' perspective that conceives of the development of transnational non-state actor communities as a function of the underlying differences in the resources available at the national level. First, our analysis supports the view that cross-national differences in global interest representation strongly favor the mobilization of wealthy countries, as we would expect based on the underlying national resource base. More specifically, our analysis shows that (i) global interest representation almost perfectly reflects differences in countries' relative economic power and (ii) non-state actors from the global south drop out at mass from global interest communities due to the limited chances they see to meaningfully interact with key decision makers. This leads us to conclude that the opening up of IOs reinforced, rather than reduced, North–South inequalities in global interest representation.

Second, our investigation suggests that global interest communities have been characterized by greater political activism by non-state actors defending domestic, rather than global, interests. In particular, our examination shows that (i) globalization and politicization, two factors that are usually thought to stimulate greater political activity by non-state actors representing global constituencies, contributed to the exponential growth of transnational interest communities, but they did not make such communities more globalized in nature, and (ii) non-state actors and government delegates from different countries hardly interact with each other at the conferences and most organizations see no value in returning to the conferences after one visit. Both findings provide little evidence in support of the hope that the rise of transnational advocacy could go hand in hand with the emergence of a global public sphere.

1 The promise of global governance?

Introduction

The observed rise of non-state actors mobilizing on a transnational basis paved the way for the development of two important normative debates about the nature and evolution of global governance. For one, scholars have started to ask what the implications of such a quantitative growth of trans-nationally mobilized non-state actors might be for *North–South inequalities*. Would the growth of transnational advocacy make global governance more representative of and accessible to all the world's citizens, or would it bring about even more inequality and exclusion? In addition, researchers started questioning whether growing patterns of transnational advocacy could be seen as tangible proof of the emergence of a *global public sphere*. Could rising transnational advocacy trigger the emergence of a global public sphere closing the gap between the global space where issues arise and the national space where such issues are managed, or rather would it lead to a global socio-political order even more dominated by the realpolitik of nation-states?

Ultimately, both sets of normative debates speak to the broader question of whether global governance can be effectively democratized. Stakeholder models of democracy posit that political systems can be made more democratically legitimate by making sure that all the actors affected by decisions produced within such systems are given the opportunity to meaningfully participate and make their voice heard in the making of such decisions. In the context of a discussion on the implications of the rise of transnational advocacy, this means that we should expect this phenomenon to bring about greater democratic legitimacy only insofar as it helps both reduce North–South inequalities and trigger the emergence of a truly global public sphere based on a fair representation of relevant global constituencies. Empirically addressing these debates, therefore, is crucial to understand whether the rise of transnational advocacy contributed to solving problems of democratic legitimacy in global governance or, rather, made them even more acute.

DOI: 10.4324/9781003246794-2

In this chapter we set the stage for the empirical discussions that will be developed in the subsequent chapters. More specifically, the bulk of this chapter is devoted to systematically outline the contours of these two important normative debates, the positions that exist within them, and the kind of evidence that would be needed to try and meaningfully assess how existing positions fare with respect to real-world patterns of non-state actors' mobilization in global governance.

The opening of IOs: toward more (in)equality in global politics?

A key normative question in interest group research concerns the biased nature of interest group communities. Influenced by Olson's (1965) and Schattschneider's (1960) seminal contributions, the scholarship on national interest group populations has paid a great deal of attention to assessing empirically whether these populations are characterized by skewed distributions of different substantive interests, focusing in particular on differences in the representation of business and other types of more diffuse societal interests (Lowery and Gray 2004). The growing importance of transnational interest group populations has triggered an interest in trying to ascertain whether Schattschneider's (1960: 65) oft-quoted claim that 'the flaw in the pluralist heaven is that the heavenly chorus often sings with a strong upper-class accent' equally applies to global advocacy.

This debate has largely focused on the question of whether transnational lobbying communities are biased in favor of wealthier countries. Is there a bias in global interest communities favoring more developed countries at the expense of poorer ones? And does the growth of transnational lobbying populations bring about ever-growing patterns of inequality and exclusion along socio-economic lines in global governance? It should come as no surprise that these questions have received a great deal of attention. Underlying these analyses is a normative concern about the possibility that patterns of political exclusion due to socio-economic factors that have been found to play such an important role at the domestic level may equally play out at the global level, effectively hindering any possibility of democratizing global governance via greater stakeholder involvement (Agné et al. 2015), and even furthering dynamics of domination over developing countries (Boswell and Chase-Dunn 2000; Chase-Dunn et al. 2000). Of course, 'input' legitimacy *per se* is not sufficient to ensure that global governance becomes more responsive to the needs and interests of poorer countries. Yet, the question of whether transnational lobbying communities are biased or not remains important because there can hardly be greater output legitimacy if poorer countries' relevant constituencies are systematically excluded or underrepresented in global governance (Hanegraaff and Poletti 2018). Addressing this question is therefore key if we are interested in ascertaining whether global governance is truly democratizing or, rather, moving toward greater oligarchization (Zürn 2014).

The relationship that exists between a country's wealth and global advocacy has been studied by both political science scholars interested in uncovering the conditions that promote the proliferation of global advocacy and normative scholars advancing the debate on the merits of different strategies of democratization of global governance. Political scientists interested in explaining cross-country variations in patterns of participation in global advocacy have long noted, in line with classical studies on interest group communities at the domestic level, that countries' socio-economic conditions are a crucial factor influencing societal groups' ability to mobilize politically and make their voice heard in global governance fora (Hanegraaff et al. 2015; Lee 2010; Nordang Uhre 2014; Ron et al. 2005; Smith and Weist 2005). For normative scholars, investigating whether differentials in countries' levels of socio-economic development promote or hinder in systematic ways countries' effective representation in global advocacy is critical to assess the long-term viability of, and the potential correctives for, a stakeholder strategy of democratization of global governance. (Macdonald 2008; Macdonald and Macdonald 2006; Scholte 2004; Steffeck et al. 2008; Tallberg and Uhlin 2012).

Existing arguments about the mechanisms that connect countries' wealth and their representation in global interest group communities suggest three broad sets of views. The first view suggests that the population of non-state actors active at the global level should have a more equitable character than the distribution of global wealth would suggest. The so-called world polity theory, for instance, argues that both governmental and nongovernmental organizations embedded in the world polity receive and transmit global models of legitimate state action. Membership in international organizations, according to this view, becomes a social imperative that is transmitted to other relevant actors, feeding back into the political process and then leading to even greater world polity ties (Boli et al. 1999). The dynamics of integration in the world polity thus generate a positive dynamic, further strengthening such processes of integration. This means that world polity ties have the potential to even out the existing differential in countries' levels of socio-economic development and, ultimately, that the growing number of international access opportunities can be expected to lead to greater parity in the breadth of non-state actors' participation in global governance among the countries of the world (Barnett and Finnemore 2004; Beckfield 2003; Boli and Thomas 1997).

From a different angle, scholars in the so-called neopluralist tradition reach similar conclusions (Lowery and Gray 2004; Falkner 2017). Neopluralism shares with the classical collective action perspective (Olson 1965) the view that some interests can more easily mobilize than others. Yet, this strand of literature highlights a number of balancing mechanisms that are inherent to the development of interest communities which ensure that, over time, representational participation in such communities becomes less skewed (Lowery and Gray 2004). For instance, initially disadvantaged groups may find ways to overcome collective action problems, thanks to creative leadership, selective incentives, wealthy patrons or sponsors, public subsidies, etc. (Hanegraaff 2015). A second balancing mechanism is the 'density dependency effect', which dampens the mobilization potential of individual interests as interest communities grow denser (Gray and Lowery 1996; Halpin and Thomas 2012). In the context of the study of transnational advocacy this means that it may be true that interest groups from wealthier countries dominated such global interest communities at the early stages of their development, but the balancing mechanisms outlined above can be expected to contribute to evening out such skewed patterns of representational participation in favor of less wealthy countries over time.

A second broad view suggests that the population of non-state actors active at the global level should largely reflect cross-country differences in the distribution of global wealth. The connection between organized interests' capacity to be active globally and their capacity to obtain resources from the direct environment in which they operate is perhaps the oldest and most widely accepted assumption in interest group research (Gray and Lowery 1996; Hanegraaff and Poletti 2020; Hanegraaff et al. 2015). In exploring the dynamics of the evolution of interest group communities at the domestic level, scholars have pointed out how their density and diversity are crucially affected by the nature of state economies (Lowery and Gray 1995). Because this relationship holds true in the national context, it can reasonably be assumed equally in the international context (Nordang Uhre 2014: 63). If it is true that more economically and socially developed states will have more extensive and diversified interest group communities at the domestic level, this should also hold at the international level. Thus, according to this view, there should be a roughly linear relationship between a country's wealth and its representation in global communities of non-state actors, with different levels of income and economic development across countries translating into roughly proportionally different levels of globally active non-state actors.

A third view posits that patterns of non-state actors' participation in global governance are characterized by systematic inequalities and that, if anything, global interest communities should grow even more unequal over time. Again, two different theoretical perspectives can substantiate this view. On the one hand, such a view is shared by scholars who conceive of the world system as a hierarchical network of nation-states bound by competitive and unequal relations (Boswell and Chase-Dunn 2000; Chase-Dunn et al. 2000). This tradition sees the world system and global governance structures as hierarchical systems established by hegemons who, because they have a material interest in maintaining a capitalist order, create and diffuse policy scripts which are ultimately instrumental to perpetuating and furthering their domination over peripheral states. Because world political organizations should be conceived as 'boards of directors for ruling states' (Chase-Dunn et al. 2000: 238), the world system theory highlights the power and inequality in non-state actors' participation among core and periphery states (Beckfield 2003; Nordang Uhre 2014).

Scholars who analyze patterns of transnational advocacy through the lenses of standard collective action theory reach similar conclusions (Braun 2012; Carpenter 2004). While focusing on the incentives and constraints interest groups face when deciding to be mobilized politically rather than on the power and inequalities of the world system, these scholars also suggest that patterns of interest representation at the international levels should be characterized by growing inequalities. Indeed, the collective action perspective holds that not only some interest groups can more easily mobilize as the interest community starts developing but also that these groups will continue to profit from these advantages throughout time. This is so because interest groups that mobilize earlier can institutionalize key advantages, i.e., achieve control over resources, gain experience, and create contacts with key policy-makers and other stakeholders, and further strengthen their position within such communities (Hanegraaff 2015; Heinz et al. 1993).

Addressing this first debate *empirically* requires answering a number of questions. First, and most obviously, it requires *mapping* which non-state actors are active in global governance in particular points in time with a view to assessing whose countries' interests are better represented: developed or developing nations. Second, it is important to consider how cross-national differences in such global communities of non-state actors evolve *over time*. Some sets of countries may be under- or over-represented at a particular point in time, but such biases can change systematically over time, making it crucial to try and detect whether and eventually which temporal trends exist. Third, an empirical assessment of how the rise of transnational advocacy affects (in)equality in global interest representation also calls for an analysis of *volatility* within these global communities of non-state actors, i.e., the extent to which non-state actors maintain their lobby efforts over time. An analysis of volatility is important, because a more stable pattern of interest representation allows interest organizations to build experience in lobbying, to create sustainable interactions with policymakers and other interest groups, and, ultimately, to increase their potential to weigh in the policymaking process. In contrast, organizations that maintain only a temporary presence are much less likely to create these vital resources. It is therefore of critical relevance whether organizations representing the interests of developed and developing countries are equally able to develop a steady lobby presence or not. We address each of these important empirical questions in Chapters 2 and 3.

The opening of IOs: toward a global public sphere?

A second important normative question related to the rise of transnational advocacy concerns its potential to trigger the emergence of a truly global public sphere, i.e., an institutionalized arena for deliberative political participation beyond the limits of national boundaries. From a normative standpoint, the question of the nature of the deliberative processes stimulated by the rise of transnational advocacy is important because it tells us something about its potential to democratize global governance. How to democratize global governance is subject to debate, and different answers have been provided to it, largely depending on different underlying views concerning the scope of the global demos (see Marchetti 2011). Some subscribe to the view that redressing the international governance democratic deficit calls for a global polity compounded by global mechanisms of electoral authorization and accountability (Marchetti 2008). Others take a less radical stance and subscribe to the view that global democracy does not mean putting in place a national democracy writ large but, more realistically, a number of institutional reforms that can facilitate the expression of citizens' concerns and that ensure some degree of responsiveness of power within global governance (Archibugi et al. 2011; Castells 2008; Held 1995; Nanz and Steffeck 2005; Scholte 2002).

According to this latter stakeholder model of democratization of global governance, the ultimate goal of opening up global governance to greater participation of non-state actors should be the creation of a global public sphere: since structures of decision-making increasingly transcend national boundaries, meaningful international deliberation requires new forms of participation of the very transnational interests affected by those political decisions. To put it differently, we can hardly expect a global socio-political order that remains defined by the realpolitik of nation-states, rather than by stakeholders that can enhance broader transnational debates, to produce democratic legitimacy (Held 2004). The argument that a flourishing global public sphere is a necessary condition for global governance to become truly democratic is central in many discussions. For Nanz and Steffeck (2004: 315), for instance, opening up global governance to greater participation by non-state actors can generate democratic legitimacy only insofar as it stimulates truly international deliberative participation. Scholte (2002: 290) suggests that democratically legitimate global governance requires overcoming nationalist structures of community and giving meaningful representation to cosmopolitan bonds and trans-border solidarities. For Castells (2008: 84), democratic legitimacy can be attained by giving voice to a truly *global* civil society, that is to stakeholders with a global or international frame of reference for their actions and goals. Others suggest that giving voice to opinions shaped independently of single national perspectives and interests is key to strengthening democracy in global governance (Dryzek 2006; Bohman 2007). Similarly, Agné et al. (2015) argue that pushing forward the empirical agenda on democracy in global governance requires focusing on how much stakeholder involvement leads to the effective representation of global interests.

This line of argumentation opens up an important question: how can we define *a priori* how a truly global public sphere should look like? Coming up with a definition is not an easy task, and, in fact, many criticized stakeholder models of democracy precisely on the grounds that it is difficult to formulate a desirable and widely acceptable ideal of democratic legitimacy. For instance, some have proposed a sociological understanding of democratic legitimacy precisely with a view to circumventing this problem, suggesting that assessing whether global governance is democratically legitimate does not mean ascertaining whether specific criteria of an ideal democracy are fulfilled, but whether stakeholders do perceive and accept as democratic the political process within which they are involved. It is beyond the scope of this work to offer a comprehensive overview of this important debate. Suffice to say here that some empirical analyses based on this sociological variant end up acknowledging that it is ultimately very difficult to neglect the question of whether stakeholder involvement is conducive to the fulfillment of particular criteria of ideal democracy (Agné et al. 2015; Dellmuth and Tallberg 2015).

We therefore seek to define a conceptual benchmark for a meaningful empirical assessment of whether actual patterns of political mobilization by non-state actors within global governance have triggered the emergence of a global public sphere. As mentioned before, it is important to stress that a global public sphere does not presuppose the existence of a global polity but, more simply, it calls for mechanisms ensuring that the relevant global stakeholders affected by decisions taken within global political systems are given the opportunity to meaningfully participate and make their voice heard in the very decision-making procedures that led to their adoption (Macdonald 2008). Having clarified that we do not equate an international public sphere with a global polity, there remains the question of what should be its key defining properties.

We believe it is fair to argue that at least two key *criteria* of global interest communities should be empirically observable in order to claim that they have triggered a global public sphere. The first criterion concerns the *geographical scope* of the constituencies that actively participate in global political processes embedded in global governance fora. This suggests that the existence of the global public sphere is conditional on the presence and active participation of non-state actors representing constituencies transcending national boundaries, i.e., that defend the interests of global, rather than national, constituencies. Hence, it seems fair to argue that the fair representation of relevant global constituencies, as opposed to a system of interest representation heavily skewed in favor of domestic ones, clearly qualifies as the first defining criterion for a global public to exist. Two opposing views exist on this debate. On one hand, many believe that the rise of transnational advocacy and the fair representation of global interests should naturally go hand in hand. If patterns of economic exchange increasingly transcend national borders, the argument goes, and then patterns of political mobilization by societal actors that are no longer confined within the boundaries of the nation-state should also become more relevant. The functionalist logic of this argument suggests that increasing externalities transcending national borders should engender the mobilization of the transnational constituencies that bear the costs of such externalities (Rosenau 1990, 1999; Haas 1975; Keohane and Nye 1977; Mattli 1999; Mattli and Woods 2009). In line with this argument, the literature provides ample evidence that organizations with a transnational organizational character may significantly affect the management of political issues within international governance fora (Glasius et al. 2005; Keck and Sikkink 1998). On the other hand, this argument has been criticized for going too directly from globalization to transnational patterns of social mobilization and thence to a global civil society (Tarrow 2001: 2). As some authors have noted, the process of globalization and the connected processes of transnational regulation are not neutral to the interests and power of dominant states (Braithwaite and Dahos 2000; Drezner 2008; Simmons 2001), and it might therefore just be equally plausible to expect globalization to foster greater political activity by national constituencies, rather than by global ones (Hanegraaff and Poletti 2017).

The second criterion to assess whether a global public sphere could emerge out of global advocacy activities is whether global non-state actors that are active in global governance are able to establish *long-standing relations*. In other words, is there contact between various types of organizations over time or are we observing mostly quick and meaningless encounters without much-sustained interaction? The consistent high volume of organizations engaged in global advocacy – and over time – seems to suggest that this is indeed the case, and there is much potential for a global public sphere to emerge. Categorizing different types of non-state actors active in global interest communities is certainly an important first step for understanding whether a global public sphere is emerging. Yet, simply the distribution of global and national non-state actors offers limited information. For instance, there may be unequal levels of mobilization within these populations across types of non-state actors, with some of them playing a central role in the policy process and others being marginalized and having no noticeable impact on decision-making (Betsill and Corell 2001; Halpin and Fraussen 2017; Heinz et al. 1993; LaPira et al. 2014). An important information to get a sense of whether such core-periphery dynamics are present within global interest communities is to assess whether there are systematic differences across types of non-state actors in terms of their level of activity over time. For instance, studies on domestic advocacy have shown that being a repeat player brings about considerable benefits such as increasing the chances of generating policy influence and, in the long-term, strengthening the organizational maintenance of organized interests (Fraussen 2014; Gray and Lowery 1996; Heinz et al. 1993). Thus, a second key important question that needs to be investigated empirically to ascertain whether a global public sphere is emerging is whether global non-state actors are able to establish a continued presence in global interest communities.

Again, it is difficult to develop clear *ex ante* predictions as to whether global or, rather, non-state actors should be more capable of establishing a continued presence in global interest communities. On the one hand, precisely because global non-state actors are created to deal with the global problems discussed within global governance fora, we should expect them to be more capable of operating within them over sustained periods of time. On the other hand, national non-state actors can be expected to face lower collective action problems and to dispose of higher organizational resources, which should make them more capable of maintaining a continued presence in global interest communities.

To sum up, the second key normative question associated with the observation that transnational advocacy is on the rise is whether it is triggering the emergence of a global public sphere. Addressing this question empirically entails looking into two sets of issues: whether global non-state actors are both fairly represented and able to maintain a sustained presence in global interest communities. We address these issues in Chapters 4 and 5.

Empirical strategy

This book's overarching aim is to carry out an empirical assessment of whether two of the major promises associated with the rise of transnational advocacy have been fulfilled. Has it increased the representation of the interests of developing countries? And has it triggered the emergence of a global public sphere? We do so in the following chapters by drawing on two sets of evidence. First, we rely on data drawn from a large-scale project (see Hanegraaff 2015) that maps all non-state actors participating in the activities of two global international venues: the World Trade Organization's (WTO) Ministerial Conferences (between 1995 and 2017) and the United Nations Climate Summits (1997–2017). Second, we rely on interviews with non-state actors' representatives carried out at the MCs of the WTO held in Geneva in 2011, Nairobi in 2015, and Buenos Aires in 2017. With regard to global climate change negotiations, we surveyed lobbyists at Conference of the Parties (COPs) held in Durban in 2011, Doha in 2012, Paris in 2015, and Bonn in 2017. We provide here some general information regarding the data collection strategy, and we defer to the details for a more specific discussion of how we use the data to address our research questions in the chapters.

With regard to Ministerial Conferences of the WTO, we focus on all non-state actors (over 2,000 in total) that were registered by the WTO-secretariat as eligible to attend and/or attended in one of the seven Ministerial Conferences the WTO organized since 1996 (see Hanegraaff et al. 2015). Basically, our unit of analysis consists of organizations which sought access to the WTO by applying to the WTO-secretariat to be accredited at one of its Ministerial Conferences. This means that our approach can be best characterized as an example of top-down mapping, whereby the mapping is strongly driven by the organizations that seek to influence policymaking processes. Such a strategy contrasts with a bottom-up approach in which organizations are mapped because they engage in some form of collective action which is potentially, but not necessarily, related to public policies. Compared to top-down mapping, a bottom-up approach is much less driven by interest organizations that use certain tactics in order to seek influence (Hanegraaff and Poletti 2021). However, bottom-up approaches depend very much on the availability of a reliable census of non-state actors, which is usually not available for international institutions. In addition, not all non-state actors willing to attend WTO Ministerial Conferences are allowed to attend. Before each Ministerial Conference non-state actors have to submit an official request, stating the reasons why they want to attend and how their interests are related to WTO issues. A small number of officials at the WTO-secretariat then decides on the basis of Article V, par. 2 of the WTO agreement whether non-state actors are eligible to attend, also taking into account logistics arrangements of the conference venue. One important criterion for the WTO-secretariat is that accredited non-state actors should be interest organizations – business associations, labor unions, NGOs, think tanks, local governments – and not individual firms. The WTO does not keep a full record of all such groups that seek attendance at Ministerial Conferences, but WTO officials who are responsible for the selection process assured us that only a small number, about 1 percent, of groups is denied access. Only for the last MC in Geneva the percentage was, according to the WTO officials we interviewed, about 10 percent. Usually, those organizations that are not eligible are organizations that seek access for reasons that are unrelated to WTO policy discussion, such as seeking a visa to access developed countries.

Moreover, it is not only the WTO-secretariat that determines who gets accredited. States that host Ministerial Conferences can also limit access, for instance, by applying strict visa requirements or has a result of their domestic legal rules with regard to non-state actors' involvement. For instance, the sharp decrease in the number of organizations participating during the Ministerial Conference in Doha (2001) was the result of the fact that fewer non-state actors asked to get access to the Ministerial Conference due to a combination of limited hotel accommodation, strict visa requirements, and the particular political climate triggered by the 9/11 terrorist attacks.

Finally, in order to compile our dataset we depended on how the WTO-secretariat stored the data. Data on the entire universe of non-state actors that requested access is not available, which implies that we cannot check potential biases in the ways the WTO-secretariat accredits non-state actors. However, it is important to note that non-state actors attending Ministerial Conferences are predominantly national ones, and that the WTO is a membership-driven organization in which different member states pursue very different policy views. We therefore see no reason why the secretariat should systematically bias its decision in favor of particular subsets of non-state actors. Moreover, as mentioned above, the percentage of non-state actors that are denied access is so low (between 1 and 10 percent) that we do not think the presence of some bias in the accreditation process would have significant effects on our results. At several of the conferences we also did surveys among non-state actors and government delegates. This allows us to gain more insights into the actual activities and views of these actors regarding the conferences.

To construct our data on the population of non-state actors attending *UN Climate Summits* we mapped all non-state actors that attended COPs between 1997 and 2011 (see Hanegraaff 2015). The dataset includes almost 8,000 non-state actors which attended one or more of the COPs since 1995. Note that this number substantially differs from those provided in earlier accounts of the COP interest group community (see Munoz-Cabre 2011; Nordang-Uhre 2014). The reason is that previous studies included only organizations which had official UNFCCC observers. One important accreditation requirement to become an observer at a climate conference is that the organization is a non-profit establishment, which excludes individual firms from registering. This, however, does not mean that firms do not attend these conferences. Quite the contrary, firms, and other ineligible organizations for that matter, often cope with these official requirements by registering as a member of an official observer delegation. For instance, Shell and the Dow Chemical Company attend as members of the World Business Council for Sustainable Development, while Siemens and Google attend as part of the Alliance to Save Energy. As the UNFCCC lists each individual participant and its affiliated organization on its website, we were able to identify all the organizations that attended the COP's meetings. This makes our overview of attendance much more encompassing and larger than those provided in earlier accounts. That is, where the former analysis identifies 1,322 organizational entities attending COPs, this dataset consists of over 8,000 unique organizations. This means that almost all organizations that want to participate, and have the means to do so, can in practice participate. This stark difference with respect to WTO registration procedures is one of the reasons that the population of non-state actors active at UN Climate Summits is considerably larger than the one active at WTO MCs. As in the case of the WTO, we also conducted extensive interviews with non-state actors and delegates. More specific details are provided in the individual chapters.

The combination of both cases provides a unique opportunity to systematically assess empirically whether two of the key initial promises associated with the opening up of IOs have been fulfilled. Both trade and environment are among the key issues non-state actors focus on and attract a wide array of types of organizations, both business and NGOs (Berkhout et al. 2017). This means we analyze *relevant* global advocacy patterns. Moreover, the fact that we have multiple sequential negotiations within both fora means that we can trace the behavior of non-state actors over long periods of time. Finally, we have data on participation rates over time, as well as specific data on the activities of organizations. This combination therefore allows us to provide a nuanced view of the role and activities of non-state actors at the two venues that we analyze.

At the same, there are also critical differences. As argued, one venue is more open to the participation of non-state actors. This means we can compare the effect of institutional differences on the participation rates of non-state actors and their behavior at the conferences. Beyond this, there is a big difference with regard to the effectiveness of these negotiations in the periods that we consider. While WTO negotiations have been *de facto* deadlocked in the past 15 years, the UN Climate Summits negotiations have produced significant progress. Especially, the Paris agreement has been one of the most impactful international agreements in recent history. This means we can compare the behavior of non-state actors at a venue in which the opening up of IOs has gone hand in hand with significant progress with respect to the content of decision-making, i.e., the UN Climate Summits, and at a venue greater access to the input of non-state actors has been accompanied with a decline of the collective decision-making capacity, i.e., the WTO MCs. Based on these arguments, we believe that these two cases allow us to develop arguments that have a relatively high level of generalizability. Because it is plausible that our results reflect broader trends of non-state actors' mobilization and strategic action within global governance, our analyses are able to shed crucial empirical light on how the opening up of IOs to the input of non-state actors affected both (in)equality in global interest representation and the dynamics of formation of a global public sphere.

Conclusion

The opening up of IOs came with much promise and optimism about the democratic nature of global decision-making procedures. In this book we systematically explore whether these promises are held or broken, that is, whether the opening up of IOs, roughly 25 years ago by now, has empowered previously marginalized countries via non-state actors. Moreover, we analyze whether the activity of global non-state actors currently meets the conditions of a global public sphere. In each of the following chapters we empirically focus on a different aspect of the two questions outlined above. In Chapters 2 and 3 we zoom in on different sets of empirical evidence on the effects of global advocacy on North–South inequalities in global interest representation. In Chapters 4 and 5 we assess whether strengthened opportunities for stakeholder involvement succeeded in enabling greater representation of global constituencies, thus triggering the emergence of a truly global public sphere. Empirically we focus on the activity of non-state actors at two key international organizations: the UNFCCC and the WTO.

2 Does global governance empower developing countries' mobilization?

Introduction

In this chapter we analyze whether the mobilization of non-state actors in global governance empowers developing countries. More specifically, we aim to assess empirically whether developed or developing countries are better represented within communities of non-state actors active at the UN Climate Summits and World Trade Organization's (WTO) Ministerial Conferences (MCs). We start by mapping the extent to which non-state actors from developing countries outnumber their counterparts from developed nations in these communities. We then analyze their activity over time: are (at the very least) non-state actors from the developing countries becoming more prominent within these communities throughout time? Moreover, do organizations come back after being active at one meeting or do they never come back? And if so, from which countries do regular participants stem from: the global North or South? By answering these questions, we provide a first macro-level view on which sets of countries are better represented within global interest communities, thus offering a benchmark to assess the relative merits of different normative positions concerning the potential of the rise of transnational advocacy in reducing North–South inequalities in global governance: a critical condition for the ability of non-state actors to empower developing countries at the conferences.

Which country's interests are represented at the conferences?

The first question we seek to answer is which sets of countries do different non-state actors represent. Our data is drawn from a large-scale project that maps all interest group participation at two international venues: the World Trade Organization's Ministerial Conferences (between 1995 and 2017) and the United Nations Climate Summits (1997–2017). Regarding the first,

DOI: 10.4324/9781003246794-3

the population of non-state actors active at WTO MCs, we coded all non-state actors that were registered by the WTO-Secretariat as eligible to attend and/or attended one of the seven Ministerial Conferences the WTO organized since 1996 (see Hanegraaff et al. 2011). In total we identified 1,962 different organizations that were eligible and/or attended at least one of the seven Ministerial Conferences. The second data source draws on the mapping of the population of non-state actors active at the UN Climate Summits (see Hanegraaff 2015). To assess the development of the COP interest group community we mapped all interest organizations that attended COPs between 1997 and 2011. The dataset includes 8,624 organizations which attended one or more of the COPs since 1995.

After the non-state actors were identified, we systematically coded them with respect to a number of dimensions relying on their websites. More specifically, 1,409 organizations active at the WTO MCs could be identified via a website offering information on their organization. We were not able to find a website for 360 organizations, but the information stored on other websites (for instance, from other non-state actors referring to the organization in question) enabled us to code at least some basic information about these organizations. It was impossible to retrieve any information for about 24 organizations. For the 972 organizations for which we could not find any website, we used the information stored on other websites, enabling us to code some of their basic organizational features. Only for a small number (121) of these organizations no information at all was found. Combining both sets of sources, our dataset includes 8,624 non-state actors which have been coded by research assistants with respect to a number of variables. These include the type of the organization, the region or countries it originates from, the issue areas in which it is active, its constituency base, and how it is organized.

For the purpose of this chapter, we coded the geographical area of the interests that the organization is *defending*. More precisely, we coded whether or not non-state actors defend the interests of constituents or businesses located in one country (i.e., national interests) or in more than one country (i.e., multilateral interests). For this chapter we rely on the coding of national and regional organizations and grouped all organizations according to the World Bank classification of income countries. We hereby make a distinction between four income groups, as defined by the World Bank. As of 1 July 2016, low-income economies (or least developed countries – LDCs) are defined as those with a gross national income (GNI) per capita, calculated using the World Bank Atlas method, of $1,025 or less in 2015; lower-middle-income economies are those with a GNI per capita between

$1,026 and $4,035; upper-middle-income economies are those with a GNI per capita between $4,036 and $12,475; high-income economies are those with a GNI per capita of $12,476 or more. We subsequently analyze how each of these income groups is represented at the UN Climate Summits and the WTO Ministerial Conferences. This approach allows us to analyze the extent to which the interests of developing countries and the interests of developed nations are represented at global negotiations. For the analysis we present below the proportion of organizations representing either one of the four income groups across the climate summits (COPs) and the WTO MCs. The results – as presented in Figure 2.1 – highlight the percentage of all non-state actors from these different sets of countries that attended any of the conferences. The black bars refer to the WTO MCs, and the white bars the UN Climate Summits.

The results paint a very clear picture regarding the degree of inequality that characterizes the population of non-state actors active at these global conferences: the overwhelming majority of the non-state actors active at these conferences represent the interests of developed nations. In fact, no less than 79 percent of all non-state actors active at the WTO MCs represent the interests of developed nations, compared to only 3 percent of non-state actors representing the interests of the least developed nations. The middle-low-income countries represent 7 percent of the population of non-state actors, and the middle-high-income countries represent 11 percent. Results concerning UN Climate Summits are almost identical: 77 percent of

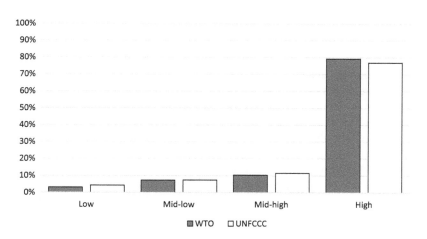

Figure 2.1 The geographical interests defended at the conferences – by the level of development country of origin. Source: Author's own data. For more information see https://janbeyers.eu/transnationaladvocacy/

non-state actors represent the interests of developed nations, only 4 percent of non-state actors represent the interests of low-income countries, while 7 percent represent the interests of low-middle-income countries, and 11 percent those of medium-high-income countries. Another notable observation is that there is hardly any difference between the MVs and the COPs. It is quite interesting to note that the distribution of non-state actors from different sets of countries is almost identical despite the fact that the registration criteria for attending negotiations in both venues differ substantially. This indicates that the distribution is quite robust and across different institutional settings and would likely be similarly observed in other institutional contexts.

This evidence provides *prima facie* support to the view that the rise of transnational advocacy has not reduced North–South inequalities in global governance, at least with respect to how developed and developing countries get to be represented within the populations of non-state actors active within it: equal distribution of organizations representing developed and developing countries. Clearly, in both institutional contexts considered, the overwhelming majority of non-state actors participating in global negotiations represented the interests of developed countries.

A potential *explanation* for this finding relates to the importance of resource availability for mobilization at the global level. Indeed, without the availability of resources it is simply not possible to buy a flight ticket and stay in a hotel for up to two weeks (the duration of most climate conferences), let alone do this on a regular basis. This view also fits theoretical accounts related to how interest group communities develop in domestic political systems (Lowery and Gray 1996) and in the European Union (Berkhout et al. 2018). Such studies highlight how the size of interest group communities is almost a perfect mirror of the amounts of resources available for organizations to become and stay active. To test whether this also applies to the development of global non-state actor communities, we plotted the relative gross domestic product (GDP) of a country, which corresponds with the availability of resources in a country, with the relative share of organizations active from this country (relative to al organizations which are active).

The results are presented in Figure 2.2, where we provide a simple bivariate distribution, with a linear trend-line, and a correlation test (y-axis indicates the share of organizations from a country; x-axis represents the share in the world economy of a country). The results highlight a very high correlation ($r = 0.815$, $p = 0.000$). This means that variance across countries' GDP (i.e., the size of a countries economy) explains the variance in the number of groups active in these countries for over 80 percent, indicating a very strong correlation between a country GDP and the number of groups active in

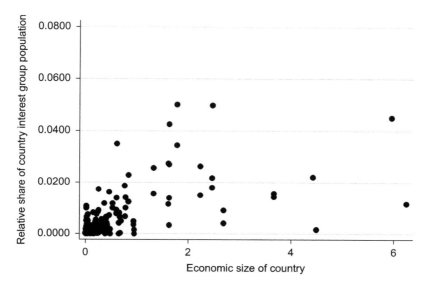

Figure 2.2 Correlation between a stake in the world economy and a stake of interest group community across countries (correlation: r=0.815, p=0.000). Source: Author's own data. For more information see https://janbeyers .eu/transnationaladvocacy/

global governance. This clearly validates our inclusion of GDP as a benchmark for how many groups we should expect to be active in global governance. In fact, almost all variations across countries in terms of the number of groups active at the two conferences are explained by one single variable (GDP), a feature we do not often observe in the social sciences. Note that the results also hold in more systematic statistical analysis, including important controls such as level of democracy, population size, government size, Gini index, and development aid (see Hanegraaff and Poletti 2021).

This finding critically shows that the availability of resources is indeed the key predictor of non-state actors' mobilization at the two IOs. In line with research in domestic politics, we highlight that it would be naïve to assume that the opening up of IOs would lead to more inequality in global politics. Rather, if anything, we would see that non-state actors from countries with much economic weight also dominate in the community of non-state actors. This confirms a supply-side logic to global advocacy where already powerful countries in global politics get more support from non-state actors compared to countries with limited global power.

Are developing countries becoming better represented over time?

The next question we ask is whether it is possible to detect over time changes in the relative representation of non-state actors from developed and developing countries. It may be the case that non-state actors from developing nations faced higher initial collective action problems but then managed to overcome these hurdles, becoming more active over time. Or, it may be that increased access to global governance disproportionally empowered non-state actors from developed countries, triggering their political activism and ultimately helping redressing, at least in part, the existing democratic deficit plaguing these institutions. In order to assess whether there is a trend toward more equality in global interest communities, we plotted the distribution of non-state actors from developed and developing countries over time. Since the mobilization of non-state actors from low-income and lower-middle-income countries is very limited, we decided to merge these two categories into one, i.e., developing nations. We compare this category to non-state actors from high-income countries, which we relabel as developed nations. The results of the longitudinal analysis are presented in Figures 2.3 (for the UN Climate Summits) and 2.4 (for the WTO MSs). These figures offer an overview of the overtime evolution of the relative weight of non-state actors from developed and developing countries in these two institutional venues.

Starting with the WTO MCs data (Figure 2.3), we observe significant changes over time: until the sixth Ministerial Conference in Hong Kong (MC6) we see a clear and overwhelming dominance of non-state actors representing developed countries. In the subsequent period, the number

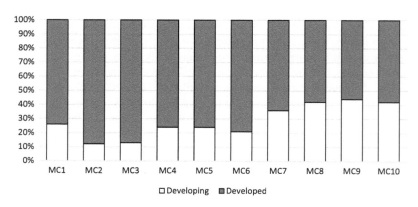

Figure 2.3 Representation of developed and developing countries at WTO MCs over time. Source: Author's own data. For more information see https://janbeyers.eu/transnationaladvocacy/

of non-state actors representing developing countries increases. More precisely, in the four final MCs there are between 35 and 40 percent of non-state actors representing the interests of developing nations. This is a clear indication that the representation of developing countries' interests improved in the population of non-state actors active at the WTO. Indeed, the time in which we start observing such an improvement, that is the Hong Kong MC in 2006, is concomitant with the crisis of WTO negotiations that continues till nowadays. As a result, while the WTO has remained very open to the participation of non-state actors, the actual participation has dropped considerably since then (see Figure 2.4). Many non-state actors started losing confidence in the possibility that negotiations would produce any significant progress and therefore decided to spend their scarce resources on mobilizing within other international political venues (Hanegraaff 2015). This is why non-state actors' attendance WTO MCs dropped substantially over the subsequent decade. This means that while developing countries' interests have become better represented over time at the WTO, in the MCs that mattered the most in terms of their potential to produce substantial policy outcomes (particularly MC3, MC5, and MC6), we see that the dominance of developed nations is still overwhelming. At these MCs, the non-state actors representing the interests of developed countries made for no less than 80 percent (MC5 and MC6), and even 90 percent at MC3 in Seattle, of the total population of non-state actors active within this institutional environment.

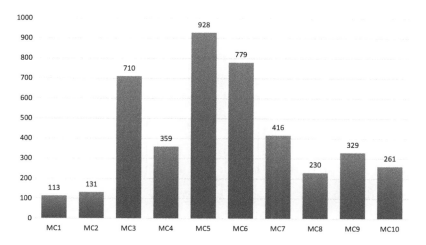

Figure 2.4 Attendance rates at Ministerial Conferences. Source: Author's own data. For more information see https://janbeyers.eu/transnationaladvocacy/

We now turn to investigate the longitudinal nature of non-state actors' representation at the UN Climate Summits. Differently from WTO MCs, negotiations at these conferences have become more, rather than less, important over time. The question we focus on, again, is whether non-state actors from developing nations have been able to increase their position in the population of non-state actors active at the UN Climate Summits over time. The results are plotted in Figure 2.5, where we can observe that there is no real progress in the relative share of non-state actors representing the interests of developing countries within this population. Rather, after an initial increase over the first few conferences in the late 1990s, we document a rather stable distribution over time with some fluctuations depending on the location of the conferences (e.g., the high attendance rate of African non-state actors at the 17th COP in South Africa) and the importance of the meetings (e.g., the relative increase of non-state actors representing developing countries at the Paris 17th COP). On average, however, 75 percent of non-state actors since 2000 have been representing the interests of developed countries, while only 25 percent represented the interest of developing countries.

The combined results of the overtime evolution in the two institutional contexts suggest that while there is some variation in the relative weight of non-state actors representing developing countries, it is difficult to identify a consistent trend. In general, it seems fair to argue that the dominance of non-state actors representing the interests of developed countries remains roughly stable over time. This is also in line with the view that supply-side

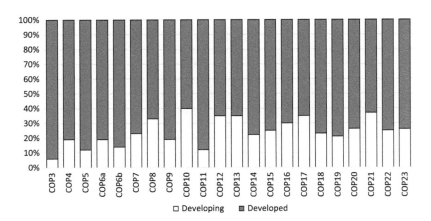

Figure 2.5 Representation of developed and developing countries at COPs over time. Source: Author's own data. For more information see https://janbeyers.eu/transnationaladvocacy/

factors (i.e., the availability of resources) are the main predictor of global advocacy patterns. The GDP of countries may fluctuate somewhat over-time, but in general these differences are rather stable and comparable across countries: Sweden does not have a smaller economic footprint than Germany in 2005 and suddenly has more economic output the year after. This is reflected in the number of non-state actors active at the IO confer-ences: the share of organizations representing developed countries should always outnumber those from developing nations, and this should stay more or less equal over time. Hence, equality among these actors is not a reasona-ble assumption, and as these analyses highlight, is not an empirical fact too.

The repeated participation of non-state actors

In our third section we analyze the volatility within this interest group community, which refers to the extent to which organizations maintain their lobby efforts over multiple MCs or COPs. An analysis of volatility is important, because a more stable pattern of interest representation allows interest organizations to build experience in lobbying and to create sustain-able interactions with policymakers and other interest groups. In contrast, organizations that maintain only a temporary presence are much less likely to create these vital resources. As Muñoz Cabré (2011: 17) argues:

> By measuring the number of new organizations, we learn nothing about continued participation from already accredited NGOs... A deeper analysis could offset this limitation with a quantitative and historic analysis of actual participation by delegates, based on the official lists of participants mentioned.

In other words, the continued participation of non-state actors in global governance could reinforce or remedy any representational skewness in the early composition of the global interest communities. In order to address this important question, we include a measure that seeks to grasp the degree to which continued participation affects the level of representation skew-ness in global populations of non-state actors. More precisely, we assume that representational skewness increases if organizations with fewer mobi-lization obstacles – i.e., business, specific, and closely aligned organizations – also develop a more continued lobby presence in global interest com-munities. In contrast, we assume that representational skewness decreases if organizations faced with more collective action problems – i.e., citizen, encompassing, and distantly aligned organizations – compensate for this lack of mobilization potential by developing a continued presence in global negotiations.

To assess continued participation, i.e., the extent to which non-state actors are able to maintain a continued presence in global negotiations, we constructed three categories that highlight the continuous attendance rates of individual organizations at the conferences. More specifically, we categorized non-state actors that attended only one conference as 'tourists', non-state actors that mobilized for up to 50 percent of the conferences after initial attendance as 'incidental participants', and non-state actors that attended more than 50 percent of the subsequent conferences after initial attendance as 'regular participants'. For the analysis of non-state actors' volatility, we excluded all organizations that were newcomers at the last three conferences, as we could not (meaningfully) predict their participation rates over a substantial number of (future) conferences. We analyze the extent to which non-state actors representing the interests of developed and developing countries fall in each of these categories. We again make a distinction between the WTO Ministerial Conferences (Figure 2.6) and the UN Climate Summits (Figure 2.7).

We start with survival rates at the Ministerial Conferences (Figure 2.5). The data shows that of all non-state actors representing the interests of developing countries the vast majority were tourists, that is attended only one conference. More precisely, no less than 73 percent of all non-state actors representing the interests of developing countries have WTO MCs only once. Moreover, 21 percent of these non-state actors were incidental participants, meaning that once they mobilize for the first time, they

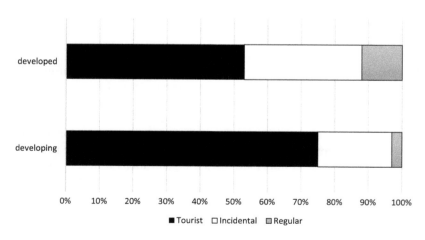

Figure 2.6 Volatility of developed and developing countries' interests at WTO.
Source: Author's own data. For more information see https://janbeyers
.eu/transnationaladvocacy/

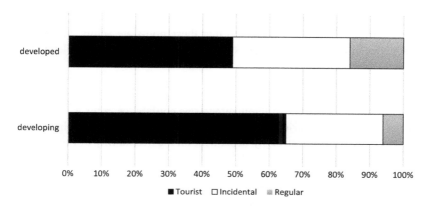

Figure 2.7 Volatility of developed and developing countries' interests at UNFCCC. Source: Author's own data. For more information see https://janbeyers .eu/transnationaladvocacy/

attended less than 50 percent of the subsequent meetings. Finally, just 6 percent of all these non-state actors attended more than 50 percent of the meetings after their first participation. In contrast, for non-state actors representing the interests of developed countries, we observe a higher degree of regular participation. While still modest, 14 percent of the non-state actors representing the interests of developed countries come back at least at 50 percent of the subsequent conferences, 31 percent of these non-state actors are incidental participants, while 55 percent are tourists (attended only once). This means that, overall, non-state actors representing the interests of developed countries are much more likely to return to subsequent meetings compared to their peers from developing nations.

Going further with the UN Climate Summits we observe a similar – but even more marked – trend. Again, the vast majority of non-state actors from developing countries are tourists (66 percent), while roughly one-third (29 percent) are incidental participants and only 6 percent are regular participants. In contrast, for non-state actors representing the interests of developed countries more regularity can be observed: 16 percent are regular participants, 49 percent are tourists, while 35 percent are incidental participants. This means that overall, non-state actors representing the interests of developed countries are more likely to return to subsequent COP meetings compared to non-state actors representing the interests of developing countries. The results, again, highlight the non-state actors representing the interests of developing countries dominate global interest communities: not only are they larger in number and remain so over time, but they display a stronger record of repeated participation. This is an important additional finding because more stable patterns of participation in these global interest communities increase the likelihood that these non-state actors will build experience in lobbying and create sustainable interactions with policymakers and other non-state actors.

Our results regarding volatility rates of non-state actors are clear: non-state actors from developed nations at both venues do not develop such experiences. They will most likely attend one conference, after which they do not repeat the experience. This finding further corroborates the view that global advocacy is strongly dependent on the availability of resources. Sustained activity at the IOs costs lots of money. Organizations from the developing world dispose of far fewer resources than those from developing ones, which makes it extremely difficult for them to maintain a sustained presence over multiple conferences. Organizations from developed nations, precisely because they dispose of more resources, can attend these global conferences more frequently if they choose to do so.

Conclusion

Some hoped that the opening up of global governance to the participation of non-state actors could help reduce North–South inequalities and, hence, increase the democratic legitimacy of these international political systems. Our results do not lend support to this view. Quite the contrary, from all the different angles we looked into this issue, empirical evidence suggests that global populations of non-state actors remain characterized by strong North–South inequalities: non-state actors that represent the interests of developed countries make the vast majority of non-state actors active in the WTO and UN Climate Summits, they remain dominant over time, and they display higher levels of continued presence. Interestingly, these patterns are consistent across the two institutional venues we analyze, suggesting that North–South inequalities in global interest representation remain stable irrespective of variations across issue areas, substantive importance of negotiations, and different accreditation requirements.

What explains these observations? What do they tell us about the drivers of non-state actors' participation in global interest communities? One important implication of our findings seems to be that the so-called demand-side explanations: explanations focusing on the resources base underlying lobbying fare better than supply-side arguments, i.e., arguments stressing the importance of political opportunity structures for lobbying, accounting for observed patterns of non-state actors' participation in global interest communities. In line with previous studies showing that national GDP is a strong predictor of cross-national differences in patterns of global interest representation (Hanegraaff and Poletti 2021; Berkhout and Hanegraaff 2019), we document that the rise of transnational advocacy has not contributed to evening out North–South inequalities in global governance. Institutional differences across different global governance fora do not seem to play a systematic role in this regard: we see similar, almost equal, patterns at the WTO and the UNFCCC. This is a strong indication that the supply logic trumps the demand logic, i.e., that resource availability is more important than institutional openness. All our evidence points out that the availability of resources (GDP) seems to be the primary predictor of lobby activity across countries leading to a strong bias to lobbyist from the global North.

Moreover, the data clearly shows that it is also not a matter of time for things to become better. Indeed, what we observe with respect to the past 25 years casts serious doubts on the optimistic claim that if we wait long enough, things are going to get better for developing countries. Our findings suggest that, quite the contrary, the situation has changed for the worse. By far most non-state actors still originate from developed nations and are actively defending the interest of the developed world. Of course, this does not necessarily mean that any institutional reform aiming to redress these biases is necessarily and always going to be ineffective. It simply has not worked thus far. It may well be the case that efforts to more systematically include non-state actors representing the interests of developing countries in global policymaking could produce more balanced results. Yet, these reforms should be specifically designed with a view to creating more opportunities for non-state actors from developing countries to match the strength of the non-state actor community from the developed world.

Obviously, an important caveat to mention is that inequality in patterns of interest representation does not necessarily mean that there is also inequality in patterns of influence. This is certainly true, yet considering that making it possible for some subsets of interests to be fairly represented is an important precondition for these interests to exert influence, these findings show no sign that the existing configuration of global interest representation could be instrumental in increasing the political weight of developing countries in global governance.

3 Inequalities in access to global policymaking?

Introduction

In this chapter we analyze more in-depth the activity of non-state actors at the two conferences. Empirical evidence clearly shows that non-state actors from developed countries vastly outnumber those of developing countries and continue to increase their dominance over time. But what happens at the meetings may still have a dampening – or even corrective – effect on these processes. For instance, if non-state actors representing developing countries gain access to policymakers more often than those representing developed countries, one could argue that opening up global governance to the input of non-state actors can still empower developing countries and increase their ability to effectively weigh in political decisions adopted within it. If, however, non-state actors representing the interests of developed countries profit the most in terms of access to policymakers, then we should conclude that the dynamics of domination suggested by the distributions we have documented in the previous chapter could be even more marked.

We tap into this important question, i.e., how much non-state actors representing the interests of different subsets of countries enjoy access to policymakers, in two ways. First, we analyze the actual behavior and opinions of *non-state actors* at these venues. This allows us to see whether non-state actors from various types of countries find equal access to policymakers and whether they believe their activities have an effect on the decision-making processes at these venues. Second, we analyze the behavior and perceptions of *policymakers* at these venues assessing whether they are open to the input of non-state actors and, if so, which non-state actors do they listen to? For both sets of issues, we rely on extensive surveys conducted at the negotiation rounds of the two institutional venues with both representatives of non-state actors and policymakers. In the remainder of the chapter we first analyze the perspective of non-state actors and then explore the perspective of policymakers.

DOI: 10.4324/9781003246794-4

The perspective of non-state actors

To get a sense of the perspective of non-state actors we rely on interviews conducted with 700 lobbyists who were active during two global negotiations. More specifically, the data were collected during six major negotiation rounds (Lucas et al. 2019). First, with respect to global trade negotiations, we surveyed lobbyists at the Ministerial Conferences (MCs) of the World Trade Organization (WTO) held in Geneva in 2011, Nairobi in 2015, and Buenos Aires in 2017. Second, with regard to global climate change negotiations, we surveyed lobbyists at the 2011 and 2012 Conferences of the Parties of the UN Framework Convention on Climate Change held in Durban in 2011, Doha in 2012, Paris in 2015, and Bonn in 2017. At these conferences, a small team of three to four research assistants randomly asked lobbyists to participate in an interview of 30 minutes. During the interviews, respondents were asked to mention a specific issue they were working on and the strategies they used to influence policymakers regarding this issue. The interviews conducted during these six conferences were combined with data collected through web surveys. Every organization that we knew was present at the conferences, based on the participants' lists, but that we did not manage to speak to, received an invitation. The surveys were sent out quickly after the conferences took place. In this way, we tried to reduce memory loss among the respondents; what happened during the conference was still fresh in their minds. Combining the on-the-spot interviews with the web survey data led to a total response rate of almost 30 percent; 900 non-state actors hailing from over 90 countries are included in the analyses for this chapter, which is the largest survey of non-state actors active in global governance currently available.

The interviews were centered around 13 policy issues for the UN Climate Summits and 17 for the WTO MCs. These issues were identified through qualitative interviews (prior to the fieldwork) with both policymakers and non-state actors, the provisional agendas of the UN Climate Summits and WTO MCs, draft agreements, position papers, and media reports. Issues, we wanted to avoid defining the issues too broad or too narrow, we kept in mind that the need of avoiding defining the policies too broadly or too narrowly. An example of a WTO issue is the future of the Doha Development Agenda (DDA). Respondents were asked whether their organization was in favor of the status quo on this issue (that is full implementation of the DDA) or whether it was advocating for small or major changes. Moreover, respondents were asked about their advocacy behavior on this issue in the year up to the conference. All the interviews centered on one specific issue, such as the future of the DDA, that was randomly selected from issues that the respondents had marked as 'important' or 'very important' at the beginning of the interview.

For the purpose of this investigation, we rely on several questions related to the behavior and perceptions of non-state actors at the conferences. We start by assessing what the objectives that non-state actors sought to pursue by attending these conferences were. During the interviews at the conferences, we asked each non-state actor representative to identify the two main reasons why they attended the conferences. Each participant could choose from a list of options concerning the reasons driving their decision to attend negotiations. The first option was to lobby or advocate on an issue of their concern. This option underscores that the main objective of attending the conference was to influence the negotiations in any shape or form. The second option was to inform their members about the negotiations. Third, respondents could indicate that their main goal was to monitor what was going on. Fourth, non-state actors could indicate that the main reason for attending the conferences was to network with other non-state actors. Finally, we included the option that non-state actors attended the conference mostly with a view to learning about the ongoing negations and how to effectively lobby. Each of the categories was identified based on prior interviews with representatives of non-state actors which had been present at WTO MCs and UN Climate Summits. The results can be found in Figure 3.1. The histograms indicate how often a category was mentioned (relative to others) by interviewees. Furthermore, we distinguish between non-state actors representing the interests of developed and developing countries.

What do the results tell us? First, we observe that the most commonly mentioned (one-third of answers) reason for attending these conferences is lobbying and advocacy. Monitoring ranked second, followed closely

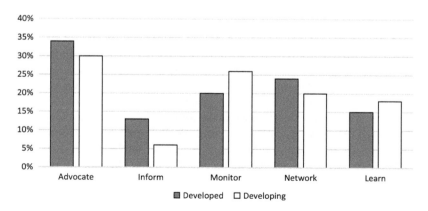

Figure 3.1 Reasons that the non-state actors attend the conferences – by the level of development country of origin. Source: Author's own data. For more information see https://janbeyers.eu/transnationaladvocacy/

by networking. Learning and informing members were the reasons for attending these conferences that were mentioned less often. Regarding the differences between developed and developing countries – our main interest in this chapter – we observe some notable differences. Perhaps, the most interesting finding is the difference between advocacy and monitoring: non-state actors representing the interest of developed countries claimed to attend the conferences to influence negotiations more than non-state actors representing the interests of developing countries did. This also fits our observations at these conferences: representatives of some large non-state actors from wealthy nations would brief other participants about their contacts with policymakers regarding the ongoing negotiations, while most non-state actor representatives we spoke to did not find any way to interact with policymakers. Rather – they indicated – they followed the negotiations from their computers, visited some side event, or read a folder from one of the stands. Hardly any of the representatives we spoke to had successfully lobbied a policymaker during the conferences.

In contrast, non-state actors representing the interests of developing non-state actors are more interested in monitoring the negotiations compared to their counterparts from developed countries. This seems in line with some observations from the previous chapter where we observed many non-state actors from developing countries were not regular attendants; that is, they attended these conferences only once or a limited number of times. While it is plausible that an organization would want to monitor how these negotiations work before deciding to take a step further and become politically active, this also means that non-state actors from developing countries hardly lobby at all. In contrast, while non-state actors from developed countries are already present in much larger numbers, each individual organization is also more engaged in lobbying and advocacy. This is yet again a clear indication that the opening up of global governance to the input of non-state actors has mostly sparked lobbying and advocacy efforts by developed countries, which further reinforces the arguments developed in the previous chapter about global interest communities being dominated by non-state actors from developed countries.

We then move to assess the behavior of the non-state actors which are politically active at these conferences, that is those non-state actors who engage in lobbying and advocacy. More specifically, focus on whether there are differences in the extent to which non-state actors that represent the interests of developed and developing countries relies on inside or outside lobbying. This is an important issue that can shed crucial light on the logics that drive lobbying activities (Beyers 2004; Dür and Mateo 2013; Hanegraaff et al. 2016; Hanegraaff and Poletti 2019; Holyoke 2003). The use of inside lobbying tends to privatize social conflict by relying on direct contacts with policymakers and making these political activities invisible to broader audiences. Outside lobbying, on the contrary, addresses policymakers indirectly and seeks to raise public awareness on particular issues. Inside lobbying is usually considered more important from the perspective of increasing non-state actors' potential to influence policymaking because it facilitates the direct exchange of the technical information with policymakers, hence the likelihood that they will be heard and affect these actors' policy preferences (Dür and Mateo 2013). On the contrary, outside lobbying is usually considered more efficient from an organizational maintenance perspective, since it effectively serves the survival-related purposes of increasing constituency support and attracting funding (Binderkrantz 2008).

We investigate this question by relying on two questions which we addressed to interviewees. First, we asked to what extent their lobby efforts at the conferences were targeted directly to policymakers, i.e., whether they engaged in inside lobbying or whether their lobbying efforts mostly focused on talking to the media, using social media postings, or participating in protest activities, i.e., engaging in outside lobbying. Figure 3.2 shows the distribution of responses between non-state actors representing developed and developing countries. The figure clearly highlights non-state actors from developed countries rely more extensively on inside lobbying strategies than their counterparts from developing countries: 65 percent of non-state actor respondents representing the interests of developed countries

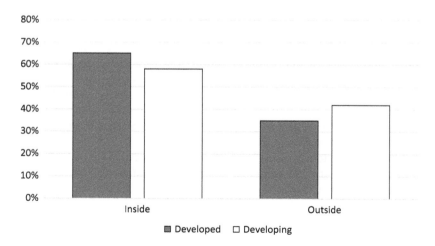

Figure 3.2 Non-state actors' level of insiderness at conferences – by level of development country of origin. Source: Author's own data. For more information see https://janbeyers.eu/transnationaladvocacy/

declared to rely on inside lobbying compared to 58 percent of non-state actor respondents representing the interests of developing countries. The opposite is true for outside lobbying: non-state actors from developing countries rely more extensively on outside lobbying than their counterparts from developed countries. These observations further underscore that non-state actors representing the interests of developed countries may be better positioned to weigh politically in global negotiations. They are larger in numbers, their attendance is more clearly driven by a desire to influence policymaking, and they rely more extensively on inside lobbying. This latter observation is particularly important because it tells us that non-state actors from developed countries tend to have more direct contacts with policymakers and may therefore enjoy a structural advantage in conveying their policy views in the policymaking process, shape policy preferences, and, ultimately, affect policy outcomes.

Finally, we also assess the extent to which non-state actors perceive to agree with the delegation of the government of their country of origin, i.e., they perceive that their policy stance is in line with the policy stance of the governmental representatives of their own country that are attending the same conference. This is an additional important indicator that gives us a sense of the insider position of non-state actors. Indeed, former research shows that non-state actors which agree with their government function as legislative subsidies for policymakers (Hall and Deardorff 2006). As a result, such organizations are much more often included in the legislative process and invited to give their opinion, and their advice is taken much more seriously. In other words, by analyzing the extent to which non-state actors from developed and developing countries support their own government we obtain additional crucial information on which subsets of non-state actors are much more likely to play a prominent role in the internal decision-making processes of these negotiations. During the interviews we asked the extent to which non-state actors agreed with their government and the results are presented in Figure 3.3. Here we see a clear division among non-state actors from developed countries, that much more often agree with their government, compared to non-state actors from developing countries, that are more often in disagreement with their governments. More specifically, 57 percent of all non-state actors representing the interests of developed countries supported the position of their government at the conferences, while 43 percent did not. The opposite seems true for non-state actors representing the interests of developing countries: only 38 percent supported their governments, while 62 percent did not. This, again, supports the argument that non-state actors from developed countries enjoy a stronger insider position in global negotiations compared to their peers from developing countries, which increases the odds that they will be able to

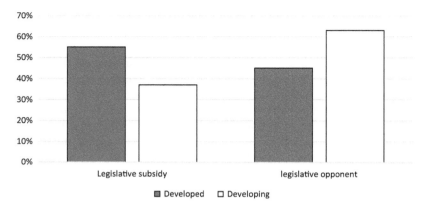

Figure 3.3 Non-state actors' relations with policymakers – by level of development country of origin. Source: Author's own data. For more information see https://janbeyers.eu/transnationaladvocacy/

weigh politically within them. Moreover, it means non-state actors and governmental representatives of developed countries tend to work in tandem, supporting each other and, therefore, exploiting organizational and political synergies to advance the interest of their countries of origin.

One of the explanations for this stark difference between non-state actors from developed and developing countries relates to the higher degree of experience the latter groups have compared to the former. As in many advocacy efforts, investing in contacts and developing a routine are crucial to developing an understanding of how to effectively advocate concerns to policymakers. One cannot simply fly in and expect to be able to be as effective as those advocates who work on particular issues all year long, have constant interactions with diplomats and policymakers, and have been at the conferences before. This, however, costs lots of money which many of these organizations do not dispose of. We have observed directly during these conferences what it means to be experienced and what it takes to afford to lobby 365 days a year. Those who have this kind of experience and resources know what they talk about, to whom their messages should be directed, and where to find relevant stakeholders. Clearly, in the vast majority of cases those possessing this experience and resources are non-state actors from wealthy countries. This stands in sharp contrast to most of the representatives we met that came from developing countries. The impression that we obtained was that these representatives had such a disadvantage in terms of preparation, contacts, and knowledge about the rules of the game that it was an unfair fight. They often participated with full enthusiasm but ended up disillusioned about what they had accomplished. The limited resources they had were spent on a flight ticket and hotel, and nothing was left to finance and take part in the types of larger advocacy campaigns that can bring about tangible results.

In short, non-state actors representing the interests of developing countries are less likely to attend the conferences in order to engage in lobbying and advocacy, they are more often outsiders than insiders, and, finally, they more often take policy stances that stand in contrast with those defended by the government representatives of their country of origin. Overall, these patterns cast light on the fact that these non-state actors do not seem to be able to compensate for their overwhelmingly lower rates of attendance rates with better access to policymakers. Quite the contrary, non-state actors representing developed countries are larger in number and seem to be systematically better positioned to work directly with policymakers and, hence, exert influence on these global policymaking processes.

The perspective of policymakers

In addition to considering the views of non-state actors' representatives, we also look into the perspective of policymakers at the conferences. The subsequent analyses rely on data collected at the same venues yet this time draw on information obtained through interviews with policymakers. As in the case of representatives of non-state actors, the team of researchers randomly interviewed government-attendees regarding their interactions non-state actors. This approach enabled us to reduce bias in the type of respondents, both with regard to the type of policymaker (diplomat, civil servant, politician) and the country they were representing. For example, government officials representing the small island-state of Sao Tomé and Principe and those representing the United States are included in our dataset. After these six conferences took place, we also conducted a web survey with participants we had not managed to speak to. Combining the on-the-spot interviews with the web survey data led to a total response rate of more than 35 percent; 297 policymakers hailing from 107 countries are included in the analyses for this chapter. The interviews were also centered on the 13 policy issues for the UN Climate Summits and 17 for the WTO MCs.

All the respondents were included in the formal national delegations of their countries with the aim of safeguarding the interests of their respective states during the negotiations taking place. This made them eligible to answer questions about their reliance on non-state actors for political and expertise-based input. Interviewing decision-makers at global diplomatic conferences provided some advantages regarding our particular question. First, it offered us the chance to talk face-to-face to a large set of decision-makers from a wide range of countries in a relatively short time span, which would not have been feasible if we had visited negotiators from so many different countries in their country of origin. Second, the interviewed decision-makers were active on similar issues in two different policy fields. This keeps much of the policy-specific idiosyncrasy under control, which increases the robustness of our findings. One could argue that some of the negotiators we interviewed had experience working at the international level and, as a consequence, could be socialized to some extent by the international context. However, we do not deem this as a problem for our argument. Indeed, even if we accept the assumption of perfect socialization at the international level, international negotiators will still have different information demands depending on the countries they come from, because these information demands are strongly driven by the countries' democratic and economic characteristics and because most information is gathered and processed in a domestic context. We therefore see socialization as a methodological advantage because it enables us to analyze the behavior of non-state actors from many different countries, while keeping constant the political venue and social environment in which they are operated (see Hanegraaff and Poletti 2017).

For this section we are again interested in contrasting the perspective of behavior of policymakers from developed and developing countries. We first analyze the overall appreciation of policymakers regarding the attendance of non-state actors at the two global negotiation forums. In order to tap into this question, we asked policymakers the following question:

> there has been some debate on whether or not non-state actors should be allowed to participate at global conferences. In general, do you find it crucial, important, useful, irrelevant, or obstructive that non-state actors are allowed to participate at these meetings?

Figure 3.4 presents the results of these questions distinguishing between the answers provided by policymakers from developed and developing countries.

First of all, the results highlight an overwhelming appreciation for the role that non-state actors play as participants in these conferences: most of the respondents view the participation of non-state actors as important (roughly 35 percent) or very important (around 42 percent). Moreover, we observe no significant differences between policymakers from developed and developing countries. Indeed, as clearly indicated by the figure, the appreciation for non-state actors' participation is almost equally distributed between policymakers from developed and developing nations. The only small difference is that policymakers from developing countries are slightly

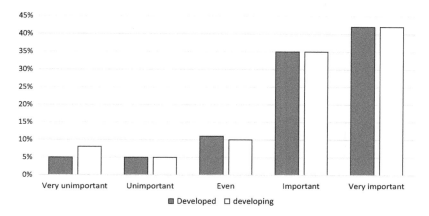

Figure 3.4 Policymakers' appreciation of non-state actors at the conferences – by level of development country of origin. Source: Author's own data. For more information see https://janbeyers.eu/transnationaladvocacy/

more likely to indicate the participation of non-state actors as very unimportant than policymakers from developed countries. Yet, this difference is very small: 5 versus 8 percent. Overall, we can conclude that policymakers from developing countries are not more positive about non-state actors' participation at the conferences than their counterparts from developed countries, indirectly suggesting that they do not consider the rise of transnational advocacy as a phenomenon that disproportionally favors developing countries. Otherwise, we should have probably found higher rates of positive appreciation of non-state actors' attendance from policymakers from developing countries' policymakers.

In addition, we investigate the frequency of contacts between policymakers and non-state actors as reported by the former. Indeed, next to the overall appreciation for non-state actors' participation at these conferences, it is important to know the extent to which they get in contact with them. Suppose, for instance, that policymakers from developing countries have more frequent contacts with non-state actors than their counterparts from developed countries, then one could plausibly argue that they are systematically more capable of actually profiting from non-state actors' attendance and input. In other words, it is one thing to claim to appreciate the participation of non-state actors; it is a different thing to actually make use of their participation during these negotiations.

In order to address this question, we asked the policymakers the extent to which they engaged with non-state actors at the conferences on a scale

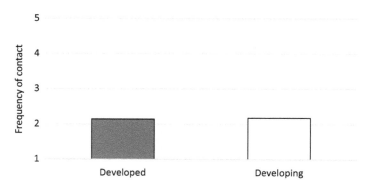

Figure 3.5 Policymakers' interactions with non-state actors at the conferences – by level of development country of origin. Source: Author's own data. For more information see https://janbeyers.eu/transnationaladvocacy/

of 1 (=never) to 5 (=very often). The answers are presented in Figure 3.5, in which we plot the average level of contacts between non-state actors and policymakers from developed and developing countries. The results paint a rather disappointing picture: neither of the two groups' policymakers actually talks to non-state actors much. On average policymakers talk to non-state actors only 'occasionally' (a score of 2.1 on a 1–5 scale). Moreover, almost 40 percent of the respondents indicate they never talked to non-state actors at the conferences. Interestingly, there are no significant differences between the two groups of policymakers: both hardly talk to non-state actors in the course of these international negotiations.

To sum up, we observe that policymakers are generally very appreciative of the attendance of non-state actors at the global conferences we analyzed, as the vast majority, irrespective of whether the represented developed or developing countries, deemed their participation as important or very important. Yet, it seems that these high rates of appreciation do not translate into equally high levels of contacts with non-state actors. In fact, quite the opposite seems to be true: the majority policymakers, again with no significant differences between the two sets of countries, actually have very limited contacts with non-state actors during these global negotiations.

Conclusion

The evidence we present in this chapter coherently complements the empirical findings of the previous one. Moving beyond a rough count of numbers to a more qualitative assessment of the views of non-state actors and policymakers does not change the picture. Non-state actors from developed countries seem to be better positioned to weigh politically in global negotiations with respect to a number of important dimensions. Relative to their peers representing the interests of developing countries, they devote resources to attend these conferences with a more pronounced interest in seeking to make a difference in terms of policy outcomes. Of course, they too are interested in monitoring policy discussions, creating networks with like-minded non-state actors and learning about lobbying practices. But their primary goal seems to be to exert some policy influence. At the same time, non-state actors representing developed countries' interests seem to have closer ties with policymakers, not only because they engage in inside lobbying more systematically but also because their lobbying efforts are more often aligned with the negotiation positions of the governmental representatives of their countries of origin.

Overall, the data we present paints a picture suggesting that non-state actors from developed countries, relative to non-state actors from developing one, enjoy a clear structural advantage in global policymaking. The results concerning the perspective of policymakers, albeit less strongly, go in a similar direction: policymakers from developed countries seem to be more appreciative of the role of non-state actors in these global conferences. This is not particularly surprising considering that non-state actors from developed countries, as documented in this chapter, tend to act and perform the role of legislative subsidies; that is they tend to work in tandem with their own governmental representatives more than their counterparts from developing countries.

Combining together the findings of this chapter with the ones presented in Chapter 2, it seems fair to argue that the expectations of those who believed that the rise of transnational advocacy could contribute to decreasing North–South inequalities have not materialized. Global interest communities remain highly unequal and are likely going to remain so in the future.

4 Has the rise of transnational advocacy triggered the emergence of a global public sphere?

Introduction

In the final two chapters of this book we analyze whether the rise of transnational advocacy has stimulated the emergence of a global public sphere, that is an institutionalized arena for deliberative political participation of global interests beyond the limits of national boundaries. From a normative standpoint, the emergence of a global public sphere could play a crucial role in redressing global governance's democratic deficit. Indeed, many have convincingly argued that such a democratic deficit could be reduced by putting in place institutional reforms that facilitate the expression of citizens' concerns and that ensure some degree of responsiveness of power within such global governance fora (Archibugi et al. 2011; Castells 2008; Held 1995; Nanz and Steffeck 2004; Scholte 2002). Since global governance implies that decision-making increasingly transcends national boundaries, meaningful and democratic deliberation would therefore call for the effective participation of the very transnational interests affected by those political decisions. To put it differently, in the absence of a truly global international sphere, hence in the presence of a global socio-political order in which political deliberation is defined by the realpolitik of nation-states, there can hardly be any democratic legitimacy.

While acknowledging that any definition of how a truly global public sphere should look like is necessarily arbitrary, in Chapter 1 we proposed a tentative conceptual benchmark that could guide us in carrying out an empirical assessment of whether or not such a global public sphere has emerged. More specifically, we identified two key *criteria* that global interest communities should display in order to support claims about the existence of a global public sphere in global governance. First, such communities should not be skewed in favor of non-state actors representing nationally defined interests and should allow for a fair *representation of relevant global constituencies*. More operatively, in our view the existence

DOI: 10.4324/9781003246794-5

of a global public sphere is conditional on the presence of global interest communities in which non-state actors representing global interests dominate non-state actors representing national interests. The second criterion is that non-state actors representing global interests should be able to establish a continued presence in global deliberations: non-state actors that are not able to sustain a *continued presence* in global governance can hardly be expected to meaningfully participate in such global deliberations and, therefore, weigh politically. In the remainder of this chapter, we start delving into these two important issues by analyzing different sets of macro-level evidence.

Criterion 1: The global nature of global advocacy

As mentioned in Chapter 1, the conventional wisdom posits a positive relationship between the representation of global interest and globalization. Globalization can be defined as a set of technological, economic, and political innovations that have drastically reduced barriers to economic, political, and cultural exchange (Drezner 2001: 53). Thus, globalization implies the deepening and thickening of patterns of exchange that transcend national borders. From a functionalist perspective, it would seem logical to expect that these processes should also trigger growing patterns of political mobilization transnationally organized societal groups. The functionalist logic underpinning this view is straightforward: as globalization generates externalities that increasingly transcend national borders, the transnational constituencies bearing the costs of such externalities should be incentivized to engage in political action within the global governance fora that are supposed to address these global phenomena. More simply, there should be a positive linear relationship between increasing global economic and political exchanges and global political mobilization (Haas 1975; Keohane and Nye 1977; Mattli 1999; Mattli and Woods 2009; Rosenau 1990, 1999).

However, this is only one potential view about the relationship that exists between globalization and global interest representation. As Tarrow (Tarrow 2001: 2) notes, such view goes too directly from globalization or to transnational social movements and thence to a global civil society because it overlooks how processes of globalization and global regulation can be affected by the interests of powerful states and national-level political mobilization. As many authors have noted, the process of globalization and the connected processes of transnational regulation are not neutral to the interests and power of dominant states, which often manage to forge the rules of such regulatory processes in line with their preferences (Braithwaite and Dahos 2000; Drezner 2008; Simmons 2001). Indeed, the dominant states in the international system have traditionally had a profound effect on transnational relations, not only by controlling non-state actors but often by subsidizing them (Uvin 2000: 15). The logical extension of this line of reasoning is that globalization cannot be necessarily expected to foster greater political activity by global constituencies but might in the end make national constituencies even more central in global politics. In fact, the idea that national interests should dominate international politics as globalization increases is very much in line with a functionalist view which conceives of processes of cooperation and coordination at the international level as the result of states' attempts to deal with various problems of strategic interdependence they face under conditions of increased globalization (Keohane and Martin 1995; Snidal 1985).

Ultimately, whether the opening of global governance to the input of non-state actors has a larger marginal effect on the representation of global or national non-state actors is an open empirical question, which we seek to address in this and in the next chapters. To analyze this, we rely on the same dataset that was presented in Chapter 2, that is a dataset of all non-state actors participated in the UN Climate Summits since 1997 and at World Trade Organization's Ministerial Conferences (WTO MCs) since 1995. As already argued, we coded all non-state actors on the basis of the information contained on their respective websites. Our first analysis relies on a specific variable: the geographical area of the interests that the non-state actor is *defending*. More specifically, we coded whether non-state actors defend the interests of constituents or businesses located in *one* country (i.e., national interests) or in *more* than one country (i.e., global interests). Initially, coders could pick one out of four options: subnational representation (e.g., Quebec); national representation (e.g., Brazil); regional representation (e.g., Asia); or global representation (more than two continents). The data was retrieved by looking at the "about" pages, policy documents listed on the websites of these organizations (see Hanegraaff et al. 2011).

For our analysis we distinguished between national non-state actors, i.e., non-state actors representing subnational or national interests, and global non-state actors, i.e., non-state actors defending regional or global interests. To give an example, on the 'about' page of Greenpeace European Unit it is stated that 'the organization is based in Brussels, where we monitor and analyze the work of the institutions of the European Union (EU), expose deficient EU policies and laws, and challenge decision-makers to implement progressive solutions.' Clearly the organization sets out to defend the interest of multiple EU countries and therefore the organization was coded as a global organization. In contrast, the 'about' page of the Canadian Steel Producers Association (CSPA) states that the organization 'is the national voice of Canada's $14B steel industry'. In this case the organization was undoubtedly defending the interests of stakeholders in only one country and was therefore coded as a national organization. This procedure was replicated for all 8,624 organizations allowing us to trace whether, over time, an increasing amount of global or national non-state actors attended the conferences.

To start with, we offer some descriptive evidence and plot the evolution of national and global non-state actors over time for both venues. Figures 4.1 (for UN Climate Summits) and 4.2 (for WTO MCs) consider the evolution over time of the percentage of national and global non-state actors attending these conferences. We start with UN Climate Summits. Figure 4.1 clearly shows that national non-state actors are more active at these conferences compared to global non-state actors. More specifically, an average of 60 percent of non-state actors were national across all conferences, while 40 percent of non-state actors were global. While one can debate whether this distribution has the potential to foster a global public sphere, what is clear is that the distribution of national and global non-state actors does not become more evenly distributed over time. Rather, we see a slight decrease in the attendance rates of global non-state actors. Regarding WTO MCs, we observe a similar, and perhaps even more marked, trend. On average national non-state actors constitute 66 percent of all active non-state actors, while only 33 percent are global non-state actors. Moreover, similar to the case of UN Climate Summits, we observe that global non-state actors have not become more active over time relative to national ones.

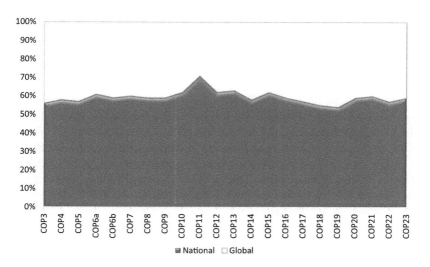

Figure 4.1 Percentage national versus global per UNFCCC-COPs. Source: Author's own data. For more information see https://janbeyers.eu/transnationalad vocacy/

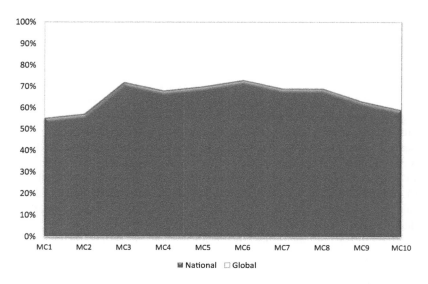

Figure 4.2 Percentage national versus global per WTO MCs. Source: Author's own data. For more information see https://janbeyers.eu/transnationalad vocacy/

In general, this evidence does not seem to support the view that the rise of transnational advocacy has triggered greater mobilization of global non-state actors. Of course, this is only descriptive evidence and it may well be argued that the potential positive effects of globalization on patterns of global advocacy may take more time to actually materialize.

In order to to further justify our claim that more collectively binding decisions with a transnational scope do not increase the potential for global deliberations, we also did a multivariate regression analysis. First of all, we want to test whether variation in world globalization over time is related to variation in the proportion of global non-state actors active at the UN Climate Summits and the WTO MCs over the years. But that is not enough. We also want to assess whether patterns of global non-state actors' activism are also affected by the level of politicization of global policy issues. At first glance, increased politicization of global governance issues could also be expected to bring about more globalized interest representation. The logic of this line or argument is essentially the same as the one developed with respect to globalization: the more collectively binding decisions with a transnational scope become relevant in public discussions, the more a transnational public sphere should emerge. As in the case of the discussion about globalizations, however, the opposite could also be true. Indeed, the politicization of global policy issues can also be expected to generate a contentious politics characterized by the confrontation between those defending transnational, de-territorialized standpoints, and those who direct their attention to international institutions to oppose, or at least use instrumentally, the migration of authority to the international level on national grounds (Hooghe and Marks 2009; Zürn 2014). Indeed, nationally oriented non-state actors can be triggered into becoming globally active when international organizations gain decision-making power and political battles are increasingly transferred to the global level. The European Union is an example of this dynamic. As Haas already argued in the late 1950s, political actors in several distinct national settings shifted their loyalties, expectations, and political activities toward a new center when European integration prospered and started making collectively binding decisions and became the object of public discussions. Moreover, several studies have shown that increased attention to EU policies and the transfer of competencies from member states to the European Union have led domestic non-state actors to increasingly shift their attention to the European Level (Klüver 2011; Dür and Mateo 2013). In short, the politicization of global institutions can also be expected to bring about greater mobilization of national non-state actors, at least relative to an environment characterized by low politicization.

When it comes to understanding systematically what are the drivers of patterns of relative political mobilization of national and global non-state actors, both globalization and politicization need to be investigated empirically. The components of our multivariate regression analysis are therefore the following. We operationalize the dependent variable as the proportion of global non-state actors active at each of the conferences (both UN Climate Summits and WTO MCs). To handle the bounded nature of this scale we use a fractional logit model with the proportion in the $(0,1)$ interval as a dependent variable (Papke and Wooldridge 1996). In order to avoid too optimistic estimates, we produce robust standard errors based on the observed raw residuals. Moreover, we rely on two main independent variables: globalization and politicization. With respect to globalization, we rely on the Globalization Index (KOF Index) by the Zurich School of Politics (Dreher 2006). The KOF Index of Globalization, available on a yearly basis for 207 countries over the period 1970–2013, measures the three main dimensions of globalization: economic, social, and political. Political globalization is measured by looking at four indicators: the embassies in foreign countries; the membership in international organizations; the participation in the UN Security Council missions department of peacekeeping operations; and the number of international treaties signed by a country. Economic globalization is measured by looking at various trade indicators and foreign investment indicators. Social globalization is based on several indicators related to personal contacts, information flows, and cultural proximity. To come to one measure, we rely on the average political globalization of all countries over the period 1995–2012.

Our second independent variable is the level of politicization. Politicization of global governance is defined as a process in which global governance generates increasing public awareness and non-state actors' contestation (Zurn 2012). The operationalization of politicization thus needs to be a combination of salience and non-state actors' conflict surrounding international organizations and/or issues being discussed at these venues. To accommodate both aspects of politicization, we combine the media attention for the negotiations per conference with the attention of non-state actors for each of the conferences. For the MCs we calculated the level of media attention by coding the number of times global trade negotiations were mentioned in World Trade Online. World Trade Online is the most used online news service for people and organizations interested in global trade. Moreover, it is a common indicator in academic research to assess the attention to global trade issues. Unfortunately, for Climate Summits we could not identify a specific news outlet dedicated to this venue. Instead, we therefore opted to code the number of times climate change negotiations were mentioned in the Financial Times. To make both data sources comparable, instead of relying on absolute hits in the news outlets, we calculated the percentage of articles dedicated to each of the individual UN Climate Summits and WTO MCs conferences, compared to all articles dedicated to either the MCs or UN Climate Summits. This way we have a relative measure of the importance of each individual conference. For the attention of non-state actors, we rely on the number of groups active at each of the conferences (see Figure 4.1). Again, to compare both venues, we take the relative share of non-state actors' participation per conference as a percentage of the number of groups active at all of the WTO MCs or UN Climate Summits. Lastly, to come to one measure for politicization we calculate the average of salience and density. To make the interpretation of our results more intuitive, we highlight the predicted probabilities plots (see Figure 4.3 and Figure 4.4).

What are the main findings? First of all, if we look at the effect of globalization (Figure 4.3), we detect a clear decrease of global non-state actors once the economy becomes more globalized. This confirms our earlier descriptive observation that the proportion of global non-state actors decreases over time, thus corroborating the arguments of those who believe that globalization and the connected processes of transnational regulation

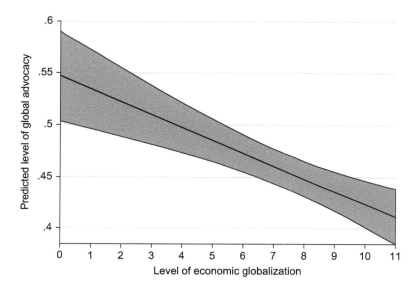

Figure 4.3 Predicted effect of globalization on global advocacy. Source: Author's own data. For more information see https://janbeyers.eu/transnationalad vocacy/

are not neutral to the interests and power of dominant states and relevant domestic actors within them (Braithwaite and Drahos 2000; Drezner 2008; Simmons 2001; Uvin 2000: 15). Indeed, we show that these broader processes reverberate into global non-state actors' communities: as the globalization of political processes increases, we observe the greater political activity of national non-state actors.

Interestingly, the analysis concerning politicization generates similar results. As Figure 4.4 shows, as conferences attract attention from the media and non-state actors, the proportion of global non-state actors decreases. From a theoretical perspective this means that Zürn's (2014: 59) expectation that increased politicization of world politics is not without risks seems accurate. As he argued, the process and results of international negotiations seem to be subject to monitoring by transnational and national publics. Even more, the politicization of international institutions seems to have generated a more contentious political arena characterized, at least, by the confrontation between those defending transnational, de-territorialized standpoints and those who direct their attention to international institutions to oppose, or at least use instrumentally, the migration of authority to the international level on national grounds (Hooghe and Marks 2009; Zürn 2014). This could

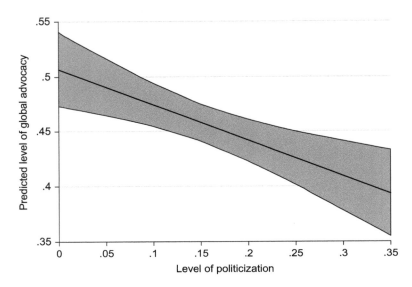

Figure 4.4 Predicted effect of politicization on global advocacy. Source: Author's own data. For more information see https://janbeyers.eu/transnationalad vocacy/

mean that the involvement of national non-state actors triggered by politicization might undermine the ability of the concerned international organizations to pursue their objectives.

Overall, the results highlight a consistent pattern in which national – not global – non-state actors are becoming more active in the two IOs we studied. Moreover, and contrary to the conventional wisdom, we found that the globalization of economies obstructs the involvement of global stakeholders in global governance. Finally, and again contrary to earlier expectations, we show that the politicization of global governance increases the representation of national interests rather than that of global ones. All these findings do not bode well for the viability of a stakeholder strategy of democratization. If it is true that the effective involvement of 'global' non-state actors in global governance is a necessary condition for a stakeholder strategy of democratization to produce democratic legitimacy, then we should be aware that existing structural conditions such as globalization and politicization, two trends that are here to stay in the foreseeable future, are running counter its success. We reflect more on the link between our findings and the potential emergence of a global public sphere in the conclusion of this chapter.

Criterion 2: Building long-term relations

As we argued above, in order to understand whether a global public sphere is emerging in global governance we also need to get a grasp of whether there are differences across different subsets of non-state actors in their ability to maintain a continued presence in such global interest communities. As in the case of our analysis of North–South inequalities, we want to also get an understanding of the extent to which global and national non-state actors differ in terms of maintaining a continued presence in global policy-making. Indeed, the analysis of activity rates of non-state actors is important because studies on domestic advocacy have taught us that being a repeat player has considerable benefits: sustained activity increases the chances of generating policy influence and in the long term tends to positively affect the organizational maintenance of organized interests (Fraussen 2014; Gray and Lowery 1996; Halpin and Jordan 2012; Heinz et al. 1993; McKay 2012). Perhaps most importantly in the context of this discussion, it seems plausible to argue that a global public sphere can only emerge when global non-state actors are able to participate *regularly* in different conferences and build long-lasting networks with similar and different non-state actors. Indeed, how could non-state actors effectively contribute to global deliberations if they are not able to maintain a sustained presence in these global negotiations? To answer this question, we first plot the overall attendance rates of individual non-state actors to get a grasp of how often they attend the conferences. In the sections thereafter we make a distinction between the survival rates of national and global organizations.

We start with the *overall* attendance rates at the COPs. Figure 4.5 plots the number of times all non-state actors attended the UN Climate Summits between 1997 and 2017, clearly demonstrating a high degree of volatility. To give a few examples, 59 percent of the non-state actors attended the conferences only once, whereas only 0.1 percent of non-state actors (or n = 19) attended all UN Climate Summits. The latter non-state actors include the usual suspects: non-state actors representing broad business associations such as BusinessEurope, the International Chamber of Commerce (ICC), the World Business Council for Sustainable Development (WBCSD), the International Gas Union, and prominent NGOs such as Greenpeace, the US Climate Action Network (CAN), the World Council of Churches, and The Nature Conservancy. There are no firms among these top 100 attendees. Yet, firms appear frequently among the most frequent attendees (more than ten appearances) and include firms for which there is much at stake, such as Shell, ExxonMobil, E.ON UK, DuPont, The British Petroleum Company, Chevron Corporation, and the Dow Chemical Company.

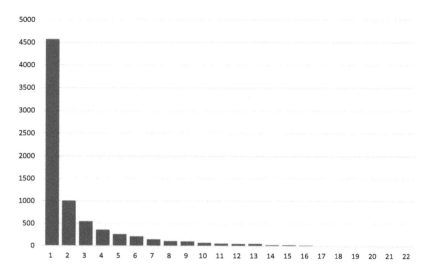

Figure 4.5 Frequency of attendances per organizations at COPs. Source: Author's own data. For more information see https://janbeyers.eu/transnationalad vocacy/

The non-state actors that had attended a large number of conferences constitute a fraction of the entire community. For instance, non-state actors that attended more than ten conferences constitute only 3 percent of the entire community. By contrast, non-state actors that attended only one or two conferences constitute no less than 72 percent, of 7,789 organizations. These organizations include a highly diverse array of non-state actors, ranging from the Indigenous Peoples' Alliance of South Sulawesi to the Japan Cement Association, and from the Montreal West United Church to the Kenya Electrical Trade and Allied Workers' Union. Generally, it seems that most non-state actors appear only sporadically at COPs and by far most of them disappear after their first attendance.

Results concerning the WTO MCs are very similar. By far most organizations attend only one conference, namely 58 percent. Nineteen percent of the organizations attend only two conferences. Combined this means that over three-quarters of the organizations have only attended one or two conferences. Only three organizations attended all conferences: Consumer Unity and Trust Society International, Oxfam International, and the Third World Network. Only seven organizations attended nine conferences: Africa Trade Network, International Institute for Sustainable Development, Public Services International, Institute for Agriculture and Trade Policy,

World Wildlife Fund, Dairy Farmers of Canada, and International Centre for Trade and Sustainable Development. It is clear that MC attendance rates are also very volatile with only a fraction of the organizations attending more than a few conferences.

The opening up of IOs to non-state actors is sometimes considered one of the most significant global developments of the past 20 years (Tallberg et al. 2014). The magnitude of this phenomenon has led several scholars to ascribe considerable importance to this phenomenon, among which the potential it holds to come to a global public sphere. However, when we analyze the extent to which non-state actors maintain a steady lobbying presence, we observe that the advocacy community at COPs is highly volatile. Almost 60 percent of the identified non-state actors attended only one conference at the WTO or the COPs, and over three-quarters attended no more than two conferences. A mere 0.1 percent of non-state actors attended all conferences, while less than 4 percent attended more than half of the conferences. This finding further challenges the ascribed significance of global advocacy mobilization. It is true, as various studies have demonstrated, that a large and diverse array of non-state actors is active at the global level (Beckfield 2003; Nordang-Uhre 2014; Schroeder et al. 2012; Smith 2005; Smith and Weist 2005; Steffeck et al. 2008), but in many instances non-state actor participation is highly unstable and volatile. In our view there is limited potential to build long-lasting networks, let alone build a global public sphere.

In the final section we analyze whether the frequency of participation at the two IOs is different among national and global organizations. For this we again plotted the number of times organizations attended either the COPs or the MCs, yet this time we make a distinction between organizations which represent national interests (black bars) and organizations which represent more than one country's interests (white bars). Note that these are relative bars, not absolute ones. As was observed in Figures 4.5 and 4.6, most organizations attend only one or two conferences. In this section we want to highlight which organizations are the infrequent and regular participants.

What do we observe? We start with the UN Climate Summits (Figure 4.7). Here we observe more frequent participants are more likely global organizations, while domestic organizations are more likely to participate only once or twice. To illustrate, of all the organizations which participate at only one Climate Summit, 68 percent is a national organization. Of the organizations which participate in all the Climate Summits, only 40 percent are national organizations. We see only a slightly different trend at the WTO MCs (Figure 4.8). During the first few WTO MCs we see a slight increase in national organizations with respect to their frequency of participation. Yet, of the organizations which have participated in at least six MCs, we

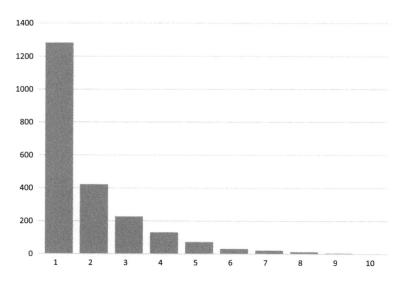

Figure 4.6 Frequency of attendances per organizations at MCs. Source: Author's own data. For more information see https://janbeyers.eu/transnationalad vocacy/

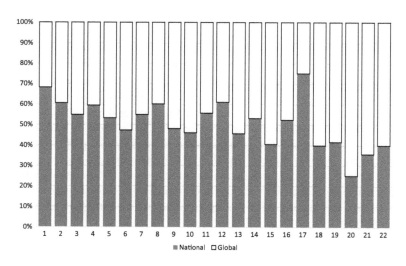

Figure 4.7 Frequency of participation by global and national organizations at COPs. Source: Author's own data. For more information see https://janbeyers .eu/transnationaladvocacy/

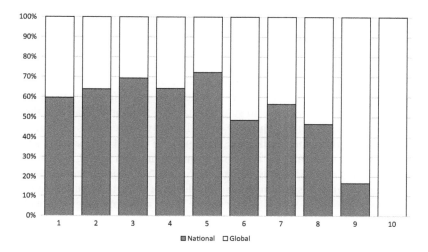

Figure 4.8 Frequency of participation by global and national organizations at MCs.
Source: Author's own data. For more information see https://janbeyers
.eu/transnationaladvocacy/

see that the percentage of national organizations declines. In other words, the most frequent participants are global organizations. Overall, this means that – while participation is limited and only a few organizations participate frequently – those which do are at least defending global issues. This holds some promise for the future. considering that the (small) core of 'insiders' at the conferences is not dominated by national interests.

Conclusion

In this chapter we explored whether a global public sphere emerged as a result of the rise of transnational advocacy. We identified two key criteria which should be fulfilled. First, the nature of interest representation should be tilted toward global non-state actors, and especially over time. Second, a public sphere only emerges if there are frequent contacts that are instrumental to developing long-lasting social connections. This chapter shows that there is little room for optimism. Despite massive attendance rates at the conferences, most organizations which are active at the conferences defend national interests. Moreover, such an imbalance favoring national non-state actors becomes even more pronounced over time, particularly when the conferences become more important in terms of outcomes. These observations clearly suggest that global advocacy is not truly global.

Our results concerning the second criterion do not make things better. By far most organizations attend the conferences only once and never come back. Only a very small set of actors attends more than five conferences (less than 5 percent), while less than 1 percent was active at all conferences. We believe this is a red flag for everyone, hoping that the opening up of IOs would lead to stronger ties among organizations and individuals. While we cannot exclude that non-state actors can develop such ties through other means, there is little evidence to suggest that it is somehow related to the activity of non-state actors. The only silver lining we observed is that most of the organizations that participate frequently in global conferences are global. This may indicate that there is a strong connection among the small core of insiders and that this is of a global nature. Yet, considering that we are talking about very small numbers, this does not seem to be sufficient to uphold the view that a global public sphere is actually emerging in global governance.

5   Is a global public sphere emerging through interactions among stakeholders?

Introduction

In the former chapter we highlighted how most activity of non-state actors in global governance remains national in nature, and increasingly so as globalization and politicization increase. Moreover, we have shown that global advocacy patterns are very volatile. By far most organizations are active at only one or two conferences. This led us to argue that the observed rise of transnational advocacy has limited potential to trigger a global public sphere. In this chapter we complement these analyses with additional micro-level evidence. More specifically, we focus on the *nature* of activities carried out by non-state actors at these conferences. This is important as it may still be the case that various non-state actors perceive that a global public sphere is in the making byway of the interactions that they are able to establish with national non-state actors of different geographical origins, as well as with global ones. To put it differently, to assess whether a global public sphere has emerged as a result of the rise of transnational advocacy, we also need to analyze the actual behavior of non-state actors when they are active in global negotiations.

In this final chapter we therefore analyze whether non-state actors and policymakers value their participation in the two sets of global negotiations in light of the two criteria for the existence of a global public sphere. In other words, why do they participate and can we meaningfully link such objectives to the emerging of a global public sphere? Moreover, we also assess whether policymakers value the participation of non-state actors, distinguishing between non-state actors from the same country of origin and from different countries. In addition, we are also interested in the actual activities which may lead to long-lasting bonds among participants, especially among participants from different countries.

DOI: 10.4324/9781003246794-6

The perspective of non-state actors

We start with the perspective of non-state actors. To analyze this important issue, we rely on the same set of data that we discussed in Chapter 3. More specifically, we use the interview data with non-state actors collected at the MCs and at the UN Climate Summits. We first seek to analyze whether non-state actors view these conferences as relevant in light of their specific participation and then zoom in on the interactions they have with each other. That is, we investigate the extent to which non-state actors have contact with non-state actors with different national origins. As said, this latter issue is particularly relevant in the context of our discussion because it would tell us there is still some potential for a global public sphere to emerge due to the fact that national non-state actors engage in global interactions that they would not otherwise have developed.

We start with the main objectives of non-state actors to participate in the conferences. In Chapter 3 we already highlighted that networking was not among the reasons to attend global negotiations that were mentioned the most (only 25 percent indicated it as one of the two main reasons to attend the conferences). Here we analyze what non-state actors indicate as the most important reason for attending these conferences. Respondents could list two of the following five items as reasons to attend either the World Trade Organization's Ministerial Conferences (WTO MCs) or the UN Climate Summits: lobby/advocacy, monitor, inform members, network, or learn. In Figure 5.1 we list what respondents mentioned as the most important reason driving their attendance. The results clearly highlight that monitoring is by far the most important reason to attend, with over 40 percent of the respondents listing it as their main reason to attend the negotiations. Networking ranks only in the fourth place, with only 9 percent of the non-state actor representatives mentioning it as the main reason to attend. In other words, the very passive activity of monitoring is considered the main reason to attend, while the key activity of building lasting networks, that is an activity that could be more directly instrumental in developing a global public sphere, is mentioned only by one out of ten respondents. This preliminary evidence does not lend support to the view that a global public sphere can emerge via intense interactions developed by different non-state actors.

At the same time, one could also argue that while networking is not the main reason why non-state actors decide to attend these global negotiations, these organizations end up networking when they decide to become active and participate in such negotiations. Indeed, when non-state actors find themselves sharing the same physical space with representatives of national non-state actors from foreign countries or with representatives of global non-state actors, they could still develop fruitful interactions that could

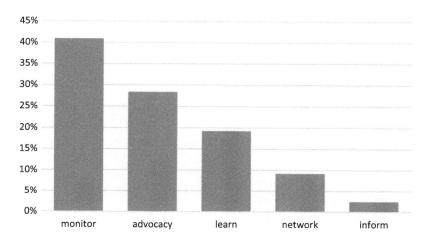

Figure 5.1 Main reasons for attending conference. Source: Author's own data. For more information see https://janbeyers.eu/transnationaladvocacy/

ultimately foster properly global political deliberations. In order to assess whether this is the case, we asked representatives of non-state actors and policymakers about their contacts with each other. In Figure 5.2, we provide the answers of the national non-state actor representative. Figure 5.3 lists the answers provided by non-state actors with respect to their interactions with policymakers.

Starting with Figure 5.2 the respondents – representatives of national organizations – could indicate how much they had been in contact with other non-state actors, distinguishing between contacts with non-state actors from the same country of origin, contacts with national non-state actors but from another country (i.e., foreign representatives), and contacts with representatives from global non-state actors. The answer categories range from very often (left side of figure) to never (right side of figure). As the figure illustrates, the bulk of interactions develops between non-state actors of the same national origin (see left black bars). In contrast, no less than 60 percent of the respondents indicated that they never (24 percent), or only seldom (37 percent), interacted with foreign non-state actors. Almost 50 percent of the non-state actors indicated that they hardly (24 percent) or never (24 percent) talked to global non-state actors during negotiations. Moreover, only 25 percent (roughly) indicated having (very) frequent contacts with foreign national non-state actors, while 35 percent had such contacts with global non-state actors. Again, there seems to be little evidence

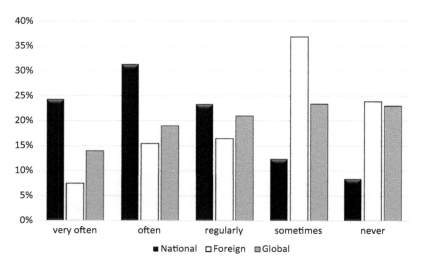

Figure 5.2 Contacts with other non-state actors. Source: Author's own data. For more information see https://janbeyers.eu/transnationaladvocacy/

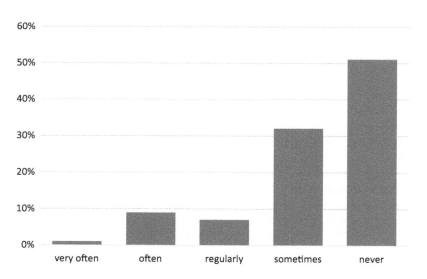

Figure 5.3 Contacts with foreign policymakers. Source: Author's own data. For more information see https://janbeyers.eu/transnationaladvocacy/

to support the argument a global public sphere may have materialized as a result of the actual interactions and deliberations developed between different types of non-state actors.

Next, we also consider the possibility that such deliberations may have come about as a result of non-state actors' interactions with foreign *policymakers*. This is indeed an alternative channel through which such global deliberative processes could materialize. We therefore asked non-state actors about their contacts with foreign governmental delegates. The answers are provided in Figure 5.3: more than half of the respondents never talked to a foreign policymaker, and 30 percent did so only occasionally. In other words, no less than 80 percent hardly had any contact with foreign governmental delegates, while less than 10 percent indicated having frequent contacts with foreign policymakers. This additional piece of evidence further corroborates the view that non-state actors have not been able to establish those cross-national networks that could be instrumental in developing the deliberative processes typical of a truly global public sphere.

What do these results tell us? Considering that (1) most non-state actors attend these global negotiations only occasionally (see Chapter 4), (2) networking is not considered an important reason to become politically active and attend these negotiations, and, finally, (3) non-state actors establish the overwhelming majority of their contacts with other non-state actors and policymakers from their own country or origin, it seems fair to conclude that the global conferences, while massively attended by non-state actors, do not provide many opportunities to non-state actors to build long-lasting relations that transcend national barriers. While occasionally these non-state actors do establish contacts and networks with global or foreign non-state actors, the number of these interactions is so small that any bold claim about the development of a global public sphere would seem overly exaggerated.

These findings are also much in line with the informal conversations we had during the conferences. While there are many people active at the conferences, most people literally sat behind their laptops, walked by the many stands that are set up at the venues, or visited a side event. Some people knew each other, but most did not. Negotiations were often held in other venues, often in hotels, and especially in areas where access for the majority of non-state actors was denied. The main conference venue was only accessible with a specific pass not available to most non-state actors. The many side-events were interesting but hardly ever led to substantive conversations with outsiders. It is therefore no surprise that the feeling we detected among the participants we met during the conferences was one of disappointment. People expected to build relations with like-minded advocates, diplomats, and politicians but ended up mostly with the few people they already knew before the conferences started. Consequentially, the large majority of the people we talked to told us that they did not intend to come back to another conference.

The perspective of policymakers

We conclude our empirical investigation with an analysis of the perspective of policymakers. Again, we rely on the same data used for the empirical examination carried out in Chapter 3, i.e., we use the data obtained through interviews with almost 300 policymakers carried out at WTO MCs and UN Climate Summits. In this particular context, we focus on the question of whether policymakers view the participation of non-state actors as relevant and, additionally, whether they actually engage in contacts with non-state actors that are not from their own country. Again, this serves as an important indication of whether the negotiations lead to (meaningful) interactions between policymakers and non-state actors from all over the world, which we deemed a necessary condition for the existence of a global public sphere.

The results are presented in Figure 5.4. Interviewed delegates could indicate the extent to which they had contacts with non-state actors during the negotiations, as well as which types of non-state actors they had contacts with. In general, the results indicate that governmental delegates had limited contacts with non-state actors of *any* type. Between 30 and 45 percent

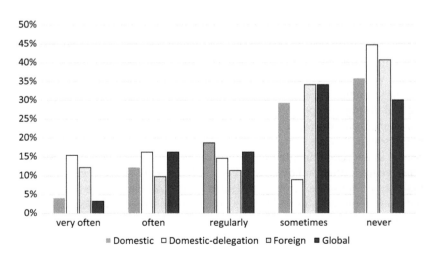

Figure 5.4 Contacts with non-state actors. Source: Author's own data. For more information see https://janbeyers.eu/transnationaladvocacy/

of the delegates indicated they had no contact with non-state actors at all. Between 4 and 15 percent only indicated they have had contacts with non-state actors very often. Moreover, considering that we are mostly interested in the contacts between governmental delegates and non-state actors of different national origin, the results look even bleaker. The vast majority of the contacts that governmental delegates had were with non-state actors from the same country, which makes for a tiny minority of all non-state actors that attend these negotiations (see Hanegraaff 2019). In short, governmental delegates hardly developed any contact with non-state actors from different countries or with global non-state actors.

These trends, again, nicely align with many casual conversations we had with policymakers, delegates, and negotiators during the conferences. Most of them were not explicitly opposed to the opening up of international organizations (IOs) and hereby allowing non-state actors to actively participate (see also the results in Chapter 3). Rather, and perhaps even more worryingly, they were mostly indifferent to the activity of non-state actors because they hardly spoke to them. Members of country delegations hardly attended the areas where non-state actors resided, while most non-state actors were not allowed to enter the parts where the diplomats and policymakers actually negotiated (if at all, as many negotiations were held in hotels of the delegations). It often seemed as two parallel worlds co-existed, one in which non-state actors operated and the other in which policymakers negotiated. True, there were some exceptions, but these concerned only the very large organizations which were often systematically embedded in delegations of their own country.

In short, looking at the perspective of policymakers further confirms the findings of the previous section: there are limited contacts between non-state actors and policymakers. Moreover, and again coherently with our previous analyses, the few contacts that do take place are between policymakers and non-state actors from the same country. This hardly qualifies as a political environment that is conducive to global deliberations that can foster a global public sphere. On the contrary, this looks more as a transposition of purely national dynamics of interest representation onto the global level.

Conclusions

We have documented that non-state actors and policymakers do not perceive themselves as being involved in global networks that could be instrumental to developing truly global political deliberations: non-state actors have limited contacts with each other, and when these contacts exist, they mostly concern national non-state actors from the same country. The kinds of interactions that would seem more potentially conducive to the emergence of a truly global public sphere, i.e., stable interactions between national non-state actors from different countries and between national and global non-state actors, are just a tiny minority of the interactions that take place among non-state actors in global governance. The same logic applies to interactions between non-state actors and policymakers. Both sets of actors confirm that they seldom interact with each other and that they mostly interact with actors from the same country.

The implications of these results are even more apparent when they are considered in combination with the evidence presented in Chapter 4. Indeed, the observations that the vast majority of non-state actors both do not attend international negotiations regularly and do not establish meaningful interactions with stakeholders from different countries forcefully combine to weaken any optimistic claim about growing transnational advocacy's potential to trigger the emergence of a truly global public sphere. If anything, our results seem to lend more support to the opposite view: the rise of transnational advocacy seems to be strengthening, rather than weakening, the representation of interests that are defined on purely national grounds within global governance.

Conclusion

The rise of transnational advocacy came with the promise of making global decision-making more democratic. Opening up global governance to the input of non-state actors was deemed by many as a policy strategy that, by giving voice to those affected by global decision-making processes, could finally make such processes more democratically legitimate. Two assumptions underpinned, more or less explicitly, this optimistic view. The first is that the rise of transnational advocacy would automatically contribute to evening out inequalities between developed and developing countries. The implicit causal logic underpinning this view can be summarized as follows: it may be true that global governance is skewed in favor of developed nations, but increasing access for non-state actors' input can rebalance existing inequalities by creating new political space for previously excluded interests to voice their concerns. In short, for many the rise of transnational advocacy promised to reduce North–South inequalities through the channel of more equal patterns of global interest representation. In other words, the opening up of IOs and the subsequent increase of global advocacy could help to empower previously marginalized countries, most importantly developing countries, thereby leading to more inclusive governance structures at the global level.

The second assumption is that, in parallel, to make developing countries' interests more prominent in global decision-making, the rise of transnational advocacy would contribute to triggering institutionalized arenas for deliberative participation beyond the limits on national boundaries that could ultimately lead to the emergence of a global public sphere. The implicit causal logic here can be summarized as follows: as problems increasingly transcend national boundaries, new transnational constituencies will mobilize politically at the global level and ultimately stimulate global deliberative processes that would no longer be held hostage to interests defined within the narrow and, therefore inadequate, confines of the nation-state. To put it more simply, the rise of transnational advocacy also promised to make

DOI: 10.4324/9781003246794-7

global governance more democratic by infusing its deliberations embedded in a truly global public sphere. This again would help to make global decision-making more inclusive and democratic.

The analyses developed in this book suggest that both promises were broken. Far from reducing North–South inequalities, opening up of global governance to more input from non-state actors seems to have contributed to further institutionalizing such inequalities. Developed countries remain overwhelmingly overrepresented in global interest communities, they display higher levels of continued presence in global negotiations, and they are better capable of establishing closer and more frequent ties with policymakers. In fact, all the indicators we used to identify how non-state actor activity affects the representation of marginalized voices in global governance suggest that the situation has not become better for developed nations. If anything, it has made their situation worse.

Similarly, more access to the input of non-state actors and their growing participation in global deliberations does not seem to have brought about a global public sphere. Despite massive attendance rates by non-state actors at these global negotiations, organizations representing national, rather than global, interests remain dominant. And it is not just about relative numbers of national and global non-state actors. It is also about the quality of the interaction taking place between these different sets of non-state actors, as well as between them and policymakers. We also documented quite systematically the minor empirical relevance of precisely these kinds of interactions that would be conducive to the emergence of a truly global public sphere. That is, participants overwhelmingly indicate a lack of stable interactions between national non-state actors across different countries and between national and global non-state actors.

What do we learn from these two broad sets of observations? The first lesson that we draw from them is that non-state actors' capacity to be active globally is ultimately a function of the underlying resource base provided by the direct national environment in which they operate. Non-state actors from developed countries are better represented in global governance for the very simple fact that they dispose of more resource – financial, organizational, and relational – that make them better equipped to become active, sustain a continued presence at the global level, and develop close ties with policymakers. In hindsight one could wonder whether it was plausible to expect otherwise in the first place. Indeed, the vast amount of empirical works on national populations of interest groups supporting this view (Gray and Lowery 1996; Lowery and Gray 2004; Hanegraaff et al. 2015; Hanegraaff and Poletti 2020; Nownes 2010; Nownes and Lipinski 2005) already suggested that the optimistic view of rising transnational advocacy's potential to reduce North–South inequalities rested on weak theoretical and empirical foundations. Overall, our analyses provide additional empirical support to a supply-side view of lobbying, which conceives of interest communities as a byproduct of the overall resource base that is potentially accessible to domestic non-state actors. Indeed, at least indirectly, our findings support the argument that more economically and socially developed states have higher levels of representation in global governance because they have more extensive and diversified interest group communities at the domestic level. The direct implication of this line of reasoning, which our empirical findings support, is that more openness in global governance is not bound to trigger the participation of formerly excluded non-state actors but, rather, to further strengthen patterns of disproportional participation favoring non-state actors from resourceful countries.

On the other end, we found little to no support for demand-side explanations, such as portrayed by political opportunity structure arguments. For instance, the patterns that we observe are almost identical across two very different institutional venues: the climate change negotiations and global trade negotiations. This suggests that our findings are not susceptible to variations across different dimensions such as the issue area, the substantive importance of negotiations, and the different accreditation requirements of the IOs. Moreover, both venues vary considerably also in terms of issues context since both venues display significant differences in the attention they received from the media and public opinion. This means that our analysis does not lend support to theories emphasizing the importance of institutional incentive structures in shaping patterns of transnational advocacy. Rather, our analyses suggest that, irrespective of the institutional structure in which they find themselves operating, more resourceful (wealthy) organizations will find a way to exploit the opportunities provided by them more than organizations which lack these resources.

The second key lesson that we draw from our work is that global governance does not automatically stimulate global political deliberations. National non-state actors dominate and are likely to continue dominating, global interest communities both in terms of the sheer number and with respect to the substantive interactions they are able to construe. Again, it seems reasonable to question the plausibility of the very logic that underpinned optimistic views about the potential of rising transnational advocacy to trigger a truly global public sphere. Indeed, many works have already questioned the plausibility of this view, both theoretically and empirically. Just as much as one could imagine global problems to trigger the mobilization of global constituencies, one could also expect the opposite: the more the political authority migrates at the global level, the more the domestic, nationally defined non-state actors can be expected to mobilize to try and counter, or at least retain some degree of control, over such political processes. The observation that growing globalization and politicization of global decision-making trigger proportionally more activism by national, rather than global, non-state actors is very much in line with this interpretation. In the context of this discussion too we find that differences across institutional venues have little effect on patterns of transnational advocacy: the way in which IOs organize meetings or structure deliberation does not seem to matter much with respect to this phenomenon's potential to trigger the emergence of a global public sphere.

Two key normative questions arise from our observations. On the one hand, one could ask whether there is something to worry about in the first place about these observations. On the other hand, and assuming that there is something to be concerned about, one could ask whether something can actually be done about it. With respect to the first issue, our answer is positive: we believe that normative concerns about the existence of inequalities in global interest representation should remain prominent within ongoing scholarly and policy discussions about global governance. We need global governance to deal with global problems, and only a democratically legitimate global governance can hope to effectively deal with the global problems that we face. If reducing inequalities in global interest representation and fostering a truly global public can be instrumental in increasing the democratic legitimacy of global governance, and we think they can be, no effort should be spared to move in these directions.

And this brings us to the second and more difficult issue. Having established that these are two desirable goals, a key question is what can be done to achieve them; hereby taking into account that former institutional reforms have not produced the desired results. The fact that attempts to increase democratic legitimacy via institutional reform have not worked so far does not mean that it might not work in the future. While access *per se* does not seem to have produced the normatively desirable goals of making global interest representation more equal and more conducive to global deliberation, it may very well be the case that more institutional reforms that combine access with more fine-tuned mechanisms geared precisely toward these two ends will prove successful.

Most importantly, our findings underscore the importance of combining a focus on reforming international institutions with a strategy that aims to tackle the deeper roots of inequality in global interest representation. Being serious about democratizing global governance requires putting money where the mouth is. If it is true that what really matters in shaping patterns of transnational advocacy is the underlying resource base provided by the direct national environment in which non-state actors operate, then redressing existing inequalities requires increasing such domestic resource base. In other words, enabling non-state actors from developing countries to fully exploit the potential to develop campaigns, monitor global negotiations, and develop global advocacy networks requires investing in support of developing countries' civil societies much more than is currently being done, and, most importantly, without strings attached favoring already wealthy countries' interests. There can hardly be equality in global negotiations if substantive underlying inequalities remain dominant. This is true for states, as we all know, but this is also true for non-state actors. Believing anything different seems naïve at best.

Bibliography

Agné, H., Dellmuth, L., and Tallberg, J. (2015). Does stakeholder involvement foster democratic legitimacy in international organizations? An empirical assessment of a normative theory. *Review of International Organizations* 10(4): 465–488.

Archibugi, D., Koenig-Archibugi, M., and Marchetti, R. (2011). Introduction: Mapping global democracy. In D. Archibugi, M. Koenig-Archibugi, and R. Marchetti (eds.), *Global Democracy: Normative and Empirical Perspectives*. Cambridge: Cambridge University Press, pp. 1–21.

Bailer, S., Bodenstein, T., and Heinrich, V. F. (2013). Explaining the strength of civil society: Evidence from cross-sectional data. *International Political Science Review* 34(3): 289–309.

Barnett, M., and Finnemore, M. (2004). *Rules for the World: International Organization in Global Politics*. Ithaca: Cornell University Press.

Beckfield, J. (2003). Inequality in the world polity: The structure of international organization. *American Sociological Review* 68(3): 401–424.

Berkhout, J., Beyers, J., Braun, C., Hanegraaff, M., and Lowery, D. (2018). Making inferences across mobilization and influence research: Comparing top-down and bottom-up mapping of interest systems. *Political Studies* 66(1): 43–62.

Berkhout, J., and Hanegraaff, M. (2019). No borders, no bias? Comparing advocacy group populations at the national and transnational levels. *Interest Groups & Advocacy* 8(3): 270–290.

Berkhout, J., Hanegraaff, M., and Braun, C. (2017). Is the EU different? Comparing the diversity of national and EU-leve systems of interest organisations. *West European Politics* 40(5): 1109–1131.

Betsill, M. M., and Corell, M. (2001). NGO influence in international environmental negotiations: a framework for analysis. *Global environmental politics* 1(4): 65–85.

Beyers, J. (2004). Voice and access: The political practices of European interest associations. *European Union Politics* 5(2): 211–240.

Binderkrantz, A. (2008). Different groups, different strategies: How interest groups pursue their political ambitions. *Scandinavian Political Studies* 31(2): 173–200.

Bischoff, I. (2003). Determinants of the increase in the number of interest groups in Western democracies: Theoretical considerations and evidence from 21 OECD countries. *Public Choice* 114(1/2): 197–218.

Bohman, J. (2007). *Democracy across Borders: From Demos to Demoi.* Cambridge, MA: MIT Press.

Boli, J., and Thomas, G. M. (1997). World culture in the world polity: A century of non-governmental organization. *American Sociological Review* 62(2): 171–190.

Boli, J., and Thomas, G. M. (1999). *Constructing World Culture: International Nongovernmental Organizations Since 1875.* Stanford University Press, Stanford.

Boswell, T., and Chase-Dunn, C. K. (2000). *The Spiral of Capitalism and Socialism: Toward Global Democracy.* Boulder, CO: Lynne Rienner Publishers.

Braithwaite, J., and Drahos, P. (2000). *Global Business Regulation.* Cambridge: Cambridge University Press.

Braun, C. (2012). The captive or the broker? Explaining public agency-interest group interactions. *Governance* 25(2): 291–314.

Carpenter, D. (2004). Protection without capture: Product approval by a politically responsive, learning regulator. *American Political Science Review* 98(4): 613–631.

Carroll, B. J., and Rasmussen, A. (2017). Cultural capital and the density of organised interests lobbying the European Parliament. *West European Politics* 40(5): 1132–1152.

Castells, M. (2008). The new public sphere: Global civil society, communication networks, and global governance. *The Annals of the American Academy of Political and Social Science* 616: 78–93.

Chase-Dunn, C., Kawano, Y., and Brewer, B. (2000). Trade globalization since 1795: Waves of integration in the world-system. *American Sociological Review* 65(1): 77–95.

Coates, D., Heckelman, J. C., and Wilson, B. (2007). Determinants of interest group formation. *Public Choice* 133(3–4): 377–391.

Dellmuth, L., and Tallberg, J. (2015). The social legitimacy of international organizations: Interest representation, institutional performance, and confidence extrapolation in the United Nations. *Review of International Studies* 41(3): 451–475.

Dreher, A. (2006). Does globalization affect growth? Evidence from a new index of globalization. *Applied Economics* 38(10): 1091–1110.

Drezner, D. (2001). Globalization and policy convergence. *International Studies Review* 3(1): 53–78.

Drezner, D. W. (2008). *All Politics is Global: Explaining International Regulatory Regimes.* Princeton: Princeton University Press.

Dryzek, J. S. (2006). *Deliberative Global Politics: Discourse and Democracy in a Divided World Cambridge.* UK: Polity Press, Cambridge.

Dür, A., and Mateo, G. (2013). Gaining access or going public? Interest group strategies in five European countries. *European Journal of Political Research* 52(5): 660–686.

Falkner, R. (2017). *Business Power and Conflict in International Environmental Politics.* New York: Palgrave MacMillan.

Fraussen, B. (2014). The visible hand of the state: On the organizational development of interest groups. *Public Administration* 92: 406–421.

Glasius, M., Kaldor, M., and Anheier, H. (eds.). (2005). *Global Civil Society 2005/2006*. London: Sage.

Gray, V., and Lowery, D. (1996). A niche theory of interest representation. *The Journal of Politics* 58(1): 91–111.

Gray, V., and Lowery, D. (2000a). *The Population Ecology of Interest Representation*. Ann Arbor: University of Michigan Press.

Gray, V., and Lowery, D. (2000b). Where do policy ideas come from? A study of Minnesota legislators and staffers. *Journal of Public Administration Research and Theory* 10(3): 573–598.

Haas, E. A. (1975). *The Obsolescence of Regional Integration Theory*. Berkeley: Institute of International Studies.

Hall, R. L., and Deardorff, A. V. (2006). Lobbying as legislative subsidy. *American Political Science Review* 100(1): 69–84.

Halpin, D. R., and Thomas, H. F. (2012). Evaluating the breadth of policy engagement by organized interests. *Public Administration* 90(3): 582–599.

Halpin, D. R., and Fraussen, B. (2017). Conceptualising the policy engagement of interest groups: Involvement, access and prominence. *European Journal of Political Research* 90(3): 723–732.

Hanegraaff, M. C. (2015). Transnational advocacy over time: Business and NGO mobilization at UN climate summits. *Global Environmental Politics* 15(1): 83–104.

Hanegraaff, M. (2019). Whose side are you on? Explaining the extent to which national interest groups support states in global politics. *Journal of Common Market Studies* 57(3): 563–579.

Hanegraaff, M., Berkhout, J., and van der Ploeg, J. (2019). Standing in a crowded room: Exploring the relation between interest group system density and access to policymakers. *Political Research Quarterly*. Online First: https://doi.org/10.1177/1065912919865938.

Hanegraaff, M., Beyers, J., and Braun, C. (2011). Open the door to more of the same? The development of interest group representation at the WTO. *World Trade Review* 10(4): 447–472.

Hanegraaff, M., Beyers, J., and De Bruycker, I. (2016). Balancing inside and outside lobbying: The political strategies of lobbyists at global diplomatic conferences. *European Journal of Political Research* 55(3): 568–588.

Hanegraaff, M., Braun, C., De Bièvre, D., and Beyers, J. (2015). The domestic and global origins of transnational advocacy: Explaining lobbying presence during WTO ministerial conferences. *Comparative Political Studies* 48(12): 1591–1621.

Hanegraaff, M., and Poletti, A. (2017). The space for civil society in the global governance of trade and environment: The cases of WTO and UN climate summits. In R. Marchetti and P. Cerny (eds.), *Partnerships in International Policy Making: Civil Society and Public Institutions in European and Global Affairs*. Basingstoke: Palgrave Macmillan.

Hanegraaff, M., and Poletti, A. (2018). The stakeholder model paradox: How the globalization of politics fuels domestic advocacy. *Review of International Studies* 44(2): 367–391.

Hanegraaff, M., and Poletti, A. (2019). Public opinion and interest groups' concerns for organizational survival. *European Political Science Review* 11(2): 125–143.

Hanegraaff, M., and Poletti, A. (2020). It's economic size, stupid! How global advocacy mirrors state power. *Regulation & Governance*. Online First: https://doi.org/10.1111/rego.12304.

Hanegraaff, M., and Poletti, A. (2021). The rise of corporate lobbying in the European Union: An agenda for future research. *Journal of Common Market Studies* 59(4): 839–855.

Hanegraaff, M., Poletti, A., and Beyers, J. (2017). Explaining lobbying styles across the Atlantic: An empirical assessment of the cultural and institutional hypotheses. *Journal of Public Policy* 37(4): 459–486.

Heinz, J. P., Laumann, E., Nelson, R. L., and Salisbury, R. H. (1993). *The Hollow Core*. Cambridge, MA: Harvard University Press.

Held, D. (1995). *Democracy and the Global Order: From the Modern State to Cosmopolitan Governance*. Cambridge: Polity Press.

Held, D. (2004). Democratic accountability and political effectiveness from a cosmopolitan perspective. *Government and Opposition* 39(2): 364–391.

Holyoke, T. T. (2003). Choosing battlegrounds: Interest group lobbying across multiple venues. *Political Research Quarterly* 56(3): 325–336.

Hooghe, L., and Marks, G. (2009). A postfunctionalist theory of European integration: From permissive consensus to constraining dissensus. *British Journal of Political Science* 39(1): 1–23.

Keck, M. E., and Sikkink, K. (1998). *Activists beyond Borders: Advocacy Networks in International Politics*. Ithaca: Cornell University Press.

Keohane, R., and Martin, L. (1995). The promise of institutionalist theory. *International Security* 20(1): 39–51.

Keohane, R., and Nye, J. (1977). *Power and Interdependence: World Politics in Transition*. New York: Little, Brown.

Klüver, H. (2011). The contextual nature of lobbying: Explaining lobbying success in the European Union. *European Union Politics* 12(4): 483–506.

LaPira, T. M., Thomas, H. F., and Baumgartner, F. R. (2014). The two worlds of lobbying: Washington lobbyists in the core and on the periphery. *Interest Groups & Advocacy* 3(3): 219–245.

Lee, T. (2010). The rise of international nongovernmental organizations: A top-down or bottom-up explanation. *Voluntas* 21(3): 393–416.

Lowery, D., and Gray, V. (1995). The population ecology of Gucci Gulch, or the natural regulation of interest group numbers in the American States. *American Journal of Political Science* 39(1): 1–29.

Lowery, D., and Gray, V. (2004). A neopluralistic perspective on research on organized interest. *Political Research Quarterly* 57(1): 163–175.

Lowery, D., Baumgartner, F. R., Berkhout, J., Berry, J. M., Halpin, D., Hojnacki, M., and Schlozman, K. L. (2015). Images of an unbiased interest group system. *Journal of European Public Policy* 22(8): 1212–1231.

Lucas, K., Hanegraaff, M., and De Bruycker, I. (2019). Lobbying the lobbyists: When and why do policymakers seek to influence advocacy groups in global governance? *Interest Groups & Advocacy* 8(2): 208–232.

Macdonald, T. (2008). *Global Stakeholder Democracy: Power and Representation beyond Liberal States*. Oxford: Oxford University Press.

Macdonald, K., and Macdonald, T. (2006). Non-electoral accountability in global politics: Strengthening democratic control within the global garment industry. *European Journal of International Law* 17(1): 89–119.

Mahoney, C., and Beckstrand, M. J. (2011). Following the money: European Union funding of civil society organizations. *Journal of Common Market Studies* 49(6): 1339–1361.

Marchetti, R. (2008). *Global Democracy: For and Against. Ethical Theory, Institutional Design and Social Struggles*. New York: Routledge.

Marchetti, R. (2011). Models of global democracy: In defense of cosmo-federalism. In D. Archibugi, M. Koenig-Archibugi, and R. Marchetti (eds.), *Global Democracy: Normative and Empirical Perspectives*. Cambridge: Cambridge University Press, pp. 22–46.

Mattli, W. (1999). *The Logic of Regional Integration: Europe and Beyond*. Cambridge: Cambridge University Press.

Mattli, W., and Woods, N. (2009). *The Politics of Global Regulation*. Princeton: Princeton University Press.

McKay, A. (2012). Buying policy? The effects of lobbyists' resources on their policy success. *Political Research Quarterly*. 65(4): 109–137.

Messer, A., Berkhout, J., and Lowery, D. (2011). The density of the EU interest system: A test of the ESA model. *British Journal of Political Science* 41(1): 161–190.

Meyer, J. (1980). The world polity and the authority of the nation-state. Studies of the modern world-system. In A. Bergesen (ed.), *Studies of the Modern World-System*. New York: Academic Press, pp. 109–137.

Muñoz Cabré, M. (2011). Issue-linkages to climate change measured through NGO participation in the UNFCCC. *Global Environmental Politics* 11(3): 10–22.

Nanz, P., and Steffek, J. (2004). Global governance, participation and the public sphere. *Government and opposition* 39(2): 314–335.

Nanz, P., and Steffek, J. (2005). Assessing the democratic quality of deliberation in international governance: criteria and research strategies. *Acta politica* 40(3): 368–383.

Nordang Uhre, A. (2014). Exploring the diversity of transnational actors in global environmental governance. *Interest Groups and Advocacy* 3(1): 59–78.

Nownes, A. (2010). Density dependent dynamics in the population of transgender interest groups in the United States, 1964–2005. *Social Science Quarterly* 91: 689–703.

Nownes, A., and Lipinski, D. (2005). The population ecology of interest group death: Gay and Lesbian rights interest groups in the United States, 1945–98. *British Journal of Political Science* 35(2): 303–319.

Olson, M. (1965). *The Logic of Collective Action: Public Goods and the Theory of Groups*. Cambridge, MA: Harvard University Press.

Papke, L. E., and Wooldridge, J. M. (1996). Econometric methods for fractional response variables with an application to 401(k) plan participation rates. *Journal of Applied Econometrics* 11(6): 619–632.

Poletti, A., and De Bièvre, D. (2016). *Judicial Politics and International Cooperation: From Disputes to Deal-Making at the World Trade Organization.* Colchester: ECPR Press.

Rasmussen, A., and Alexandrova, P. (2012). Foreign interests lobbying Brussels: Participation of Non-EU members in commission consultations. *Journal of Common Market Studies* 50(4): 614–631.

Rasmussen, A., and Carroll, B. J. (2014). Determinants of upper-class dominance in the heavenly chorus: Lessons from European Union online consultations. *British Journal of Political Science* 44(2): 445–459.

Rohrschneider, R., and Dalton, R. (2002). A global network? Transnational cooperation among environmental groups. *Journal of Politics* 64: 510–533.

Ron, J., Ramos, H., and Rodgers, K. (2005). Transnational information politics. NGO human rights reporting, 1986–2000. *International Studies Quarterly* 49: 557–587.

Rosenau, J. (1990). *Turbulence in World Politics A Theory of Change and Continuity.* Princeton: Princeton University Press.

Rosenau, J. (1999). Towards and ontology for global governance. In M. Hewson and T. J. Sinclair (eds.), *Approaches to Global Governance Theory.* Albany: State University of New York Press, pp. 293.

Schattschneider, E. E. (1960). *The Semisovereign People.* New York: Holt, Rinehart, and Winston.

Scholte, J. A. (2002). Civil society and democracy in global governance. *Global Governance* 8(3): 281–304.

Scholte, J. A. (2004). Civil society and democratically accountable global governance. *Government and Opposition* 39(2): 211–233.

Schroeder, H., Boykoff, M. T., and Spiers, L. (2012). Equity and state representations in climate negotiations. *Nature Climate Change* 2(12): 834–836.

Simmons, B. (2001). International politics of harmonization: The case of capital market regulation. *International Organization* 55: 589–620.

Smith, J. (2005). Globalization and transnational social movement organizations. In G. F. Davis, D. McAdam, R. W. Scott, and M. N. Zald (eds.), *Social Movements and Organization Theory.* Cambridge: Cambridge University Press.

Smith, J., and Weist, D. (2005). The uneven geography of global civil society: National and global influences on transnational association. *Social Forces* 84(2): 621–652.

Snidal, D. (1985). Coordination versus prisoners' dilemma: Implications for international cooperation and regimes. *American Political Science Review* 79(4): 923–942.

Steffeck, J., Kissling, C., and Nanz, P. (eds.). (2008). *Civil Society Participation in European and Global Governance: A Cure for the Democratic Deficit?* Basingstoke: Palgrave Macmillan.

Stroup, S., and Murdie, A. (2012). There's no place like home: Explaining international NGO advocacy. *Review of International Organizations* 7(4): 425–448.

Tallberg, J., and Uhlin, A. (2012). Civil society and global democracy: An assessment. In D. Archibugi, M. Koenig-Archibugi, and R. Marchetti (eds.), *Global Democracy: Normative and Empirical Perspectives.* Cambridge: Cambridge University Press, pp. 210–232.

Tallberg, J., Sommerer, T., Squatrito, T., and Jönsson, C. (2013). *The Opening Up of International Organizations: Transnational Access in Global Governance.* Cambridge: Cambridge University Press.

Tallberg, J., Sommerer, T., Squatrito, T., and Jönsson, C. (2014). Explaining the transnational design of international organizations. *International Organization* 68(4): 741–774.

Tarrow, S. (2001). Transnational politics: Contention and institutions in international politics. *Annual Review of Political Science* 4(1): 1–20.

Uvin, P. (2000). From local organizations to global governance: The role of NGOs in international relations. In K. Stukes (ed.), *Global Institutions and Global Empowerment: Competing Theoretical Perspectives.* New York: St. Martins, pp. 9–29.

Zürn, M. (2014). The politicization of world politics and its effects: Eight propositions. *European Political Science Review* 6: 47–71.

Index

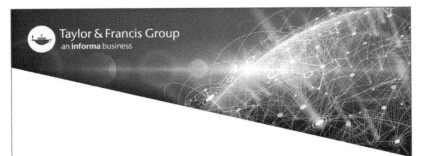